She Makes More

Inside the Minds of Female Breadwinners

by Dr. Dawn DeLavallade

She Makes More:
Inside the Minds of Female Breadwinners
This book includes interviews with subjects whose names have been changed to protect their identity.

Copyright © 2012 by Dawn DeLavallade, M.D.
All rights reserved.

This book is protected under the copyright laws of the United States of America. Any reproduction or other unauthorized use of the material or artwork herein is prohibited without the express written permission of the author.

To Contact the Author:
www.shemakesmore.com
dawn@shemakesmore.com

ISBN-13: 978-1478207504
ISBN-10: 1478207507

First Printing: September 2012
Printed in the United States of America.

Typesetting/Interior Layout Design:
Giánna Perada
Bright Eyes
www.brighteyes.org

Cover Design:
Jim Battista
Troywil Advertising & Design
www.troywil.com

Dedications

In memory of...

My grandmother, Blanche Turner. Your hand is on the throttle and your eyes are on the rail.

My life coach, Mr. Al Lewis. You made me slow down long enough to dream. Your words will always be remembered!

Dedicated to...

My husband and son, Ty and Ty. I love you both. Thank you for joining me on this journey called "God's Plan." We have never looked back!

Special thanks...

My sister-friend, Dr. Stacy Garrett Ray. I hope our creative paths cross again in the future and we can create more magic!

The Author's Disclaimer

WHY DO I FEEL THE need to have a disclaimer? Because some of the concepts contained in this book have been difficult for me to write, and will be equally as difficult to receive. I need to clarify a few things right up front regarding my goals and motives for writing this book. First, I am not a rabble-rouser and I receive no pleasure from stirring up trouble. I am a wife, a mother, a physician, and now I am an author. I was born with an undeniable tendency to speak the truth, particularly when the absence of truth is causing more harm than good. I have been blessed with many things and **one of those is insight—the capacity to discern the true nature of** a situation. My insight tells me that we are witnessing the greatest experiment in gender relations since Adam and Eve.

We can sit back and passively watch the rise of female breadwinners and its effects on the institution of marriage, or we can get engaged to bring about a positive outcome. If left to our own **devices, an unhealthy gender struggle may ensue which has the** potential to deteriorate the institution of marriage as we know it. If we as a society fail to pro-actively participate in the phenomenon of the rise of female breadwinners, we will all lose. This book is my attempt to do my part. In a productive conversation, only one person can talk at a time. Therefore, I am starting with the female point of view. While many of the concepts in this book can feel hurtful and pejorative, they are based on honest thoughts and feelings expressed by female breadwinners. America can no longer keep its head in the sand. We must face some of the ugly truths contained in these relationships so that we can move toward a solution. *Don't kill the messenger!*

Contents

Dedications 3
The Author's Disclaimer 4
Foreword 7
Chapter One: The History of Her Story 11
Chapter Two: The Perfect Storm 21
Chapter Three: The Interviews 27
Chapter Four: A Good Leader is Hard to Find 159
Chapter Five: I Swear to Tell the Whole Truth and
    Nothing but Half the Truth! 173
Chapter Six: Sending Out an S.O.S. 179
Chapter Seven: When Life Hands You Lemons 207
Chapter Eight: Dr. Jekyll & Mrs. Hyde 213
Chapter Nine: Damaged Goods 221
Chapter Ten: You Can't Eat Love for Dinner 229
Chapter Eleven: The Covenant, The Virtue of Fairness ... 239
Chapter Twelve: Sow Your Seeds,
    The Virtue of Financial Literacy 245
Chapter Thirteen: Do the Hustle, The Virtue of Sacrifice ... 253
Chapter Fourteen: Mantrum, The Man Tantrum 261
Closing Thoughts: Where Do We Go From Here? 267
Bringing About Healthy Change 269

Foreword

WHEN YOU LOOK AT A heterosexual couple, social tradition tells you that the male before you is the provider of the greater income. Well for 1 in 4 of those couples in the new millennium, you would be utterly wrong. "Female Breadwinner" describes the newest breed of American wife. Despite her increasing presence in American marriages, **the female breadwinner remains a nameless** and faceless figure within the American psyche. This book will properly introduce Female Breadwinners to America, exposing never-revealed secrets about how "out-earning" their men makes them think and feel.

There is a familiar quote in the American lexicon made **famous by Eldridge Cleaver in a 1968 speech which states**, "If you're not a part of the solution, then you're a part of the problem." On June 6, 2010, I decided I would no longer be a part of the problem. My purpose for writing this book is a simple one, to improve the course of American relationships over the next several decades. I recognize that this sounds like a daunting task, but it's not daunting at all if you acknowledge the importance of communication in the success and health of relationships. The role of female breadwinner is not an easy one, I know this first-hand in my own marriage. I have missed opportunities for effective communication and have therefore missed opportunities to move toward growth. This book is my attempt to make things right. I want to make things right, not just for myself but for the millions of other female breadwinners in this country. This book is the beginning of my journey toward a solution.

Within the pages of this book are many hidden truths; truths that will be revealed not in an attempt to create division, competition, or to point blame. Instead, truths will be revealed in accordance with a spirit of healing, understanding, and honesty. The topic of female breadwinners is a brand new concept for some sectors of our society and may seem like old news to others. America is a melting pot of cultures, ideals, marital rituals, and expectations. Our expectations of the roles of husband and wife in a marriage stem from our experiences growing up—what we witnessed in our parents' relationships, what we saw on television, or what we may have read in books. Many youngsters were as influenced by the domesticated icon, June Cleaver, from the popular television show Leave It to Beaver as they were by their own mother's behavior.

The adult love relationships we witnessed during our formative years guide our expectations regarding gender roles in our own marriages. Our concept of what a husband should be likely stemmed to a great degree from the behaviors that our own fathers displayed. When we saw our mothers cooking Sunday dinners, our expectation of a woman's role in a marriage were being formulated right before us.

A journey toward truth must begin with accurate accounts and experiences from women who have first-hand experience as the higher-earning wife. Our topic of how marriages are affected when the wife earns more is a broad one; the male and female perspectives are bound to be vastly different. Only through honest testimony, communication, and exchange of ideas can these differences be revealed so that we as a society may move toward a solution. Although the topic will ruffle a lot of feathers, the purpose of this book is not to provoke a gender war! On the contrary, the purpose of this book is to strengthen the union between partners in a marriage containing a female breadwinner.

A new equilibrium between genders is on the horizon. I hope this book will serve as a catalyst, initiating honest dialogue between the sexes. The data revealed in this book will inspire couples to finally engage in effective communication **about a topic which can be extremely uncomfortable to dis**cuss. The presence of a female breadwinner in a marriage can be damaging to the male ego; after all, many men associate money with power. When in relationships with a female **who is the higher earner, how do men go about maintaining** the power that they feel entitled to as the males in that relationship?

Despite the tenuous nature of this topic, our culture must confront this topic head-on; this trend of female breadwinners is becoming more commonplace with each passing year. The January 2012 issue of Bloomberg Businessweek reads, "This role reversal is occurring more and more as women edge past men at work. Women now fill a majority of jobs in the U.S." In addition, this issue revealed that 54% of college graduates are women. Considering these statistics, one can only deduce that this relationship dynamic will continue to gain prevalence over the next century. America can no longer **ignore the presence of female breadwinners!**

Using a journalistic approach, several female breadwinners were interviewed for the purposes of this book. These subjects represent a diverse cohort of women who are the breadwinners in their marriages. Despite the fact that these **women represent a variety of races and demographics, they** share a common bond. They are all faced with a non-traditional income profile within their marriages. Even in today's more liberal society, there remains a very viable undercurrent of shame and secrecy about breadwinning wives. With no role models to mimic, these ladies have had to act as trailblazers, navigating their way through a unique circumstance; a circumstance that has its fair share of challenges and rewards. Some of these ladies' marriages have succeeded and some have failed. I have included all of their stories here. Their names have been changed to protect their identity. These women's candid and riveting testimonies will shape our journey toward truth, and will move us one step closer to a place of understanding and acceptance. My passion is to provide a voice for female breadwinners across America in an effort to help marriages containing a female breadwinner survive and thrive.

Chapter One
The History of Her Story

TO CLEARLY UNDERSTAND THE FEMALE breadwinner, it is fitting to recount the history of women in the American workforce because it provides a framework for where we are today. This history is one riddled with struggle, discrimination, and perseverance on the part of American women since the nineteenth century. Upon reviewing the events leading up to today's statistics (women comprising 50% of the workforce in the millennium), it becomes quite **evident that women have been treated less than fairly by the** U.S. labor force throughout American history. Women have been systematically lured into and subsequently shuffled out of the American labor force as well as institutions of higher learning since their first experiences working outside of the home during the mid-1800s. Women in the workforce have **been manipulated like pawns in response to the economic** climate and political agenda of America.

Before the American Revolution of late 18th century, women received a smattering of education in "dame schools" but were forbidden from attending college preparatory schools and certain "common schools." It wasn't until after the American Revolution that any importance was placed on educating girls as well as boys. And even then, the ulterior motive for increasing the educational experience of girls "was simply to make a woman's life happier and more efficient as a wife and mother. The reason that education for women was given a boost after the Revolution was strictly utilitarian: women who were educated in the right way would be able to run a home more smoothly and, more importantly, steer their husbands and sons in the direction of sound moral development."[1]

After the Civil War, there was an increased popularity in common schools providing children with instruction in arithmetic, writing, and reading. The male segment of society was encouraged to start businesses and become entrepreneurs as opposed to earning liberal arts degrees in college which would have secured a path in teaching. After the war, there was increased federal funding for colleges and institutions of higher education. There was also an increase in endowments for private institutions of higher learning. Preoccupied with entrepreneurial pursuits, the male segment of the population failed to enroll and fill the blossoming college positions. Men were turning their noses up at the low pay of teaching positions as well as the low-status affiliated with this career path.

By the middle of the 19th century, colleges allowing women to enroll were becoming more commonplace across the nation. Oberlin College in Ohio was one of the first institutions to provide higher learning for women and African Americans. The main goal of these schools was to prepare women to enter the teaching profession and reverse the teacher shortage that had developed across the United States. As an act of national importance, women were encouraged to fill these positions to meet the increasing educational needs of

---

[1] Gloria Danzinger and Rita J.Simon, *Women's Movement in America- Their Successes, Disappointments, and Aspirations* (New York: Praeger, 1991) 39.

the next generation. Women embraced this opportunity for education and accepted these low-paying teaching positions; **this series of events would serve to establish teaching as a** predominately female profession for decades to come. These circumstances essentially marked the beginning of significant contributions by women to the American workforce.

Fast-forward to the Great Depression of the 1930s, which is frequently attributed to financial irresponsibility and a major Wall Street crash. As a result, the country was plagued with high unemployment, poverty, and deflation. These economic constraints forced the U.S. government to institute widespread restrictions on citizen employment. **Available wages were so limited that the government needed to** ensure that citizen employment was divided equally across households. In an effort to ration wages, they put forth rules stating that only one adult member of each household could be employed in the federal civil service. It's no surprise that women represented the overwhelming majority of workers who were fired from their federal jobs.

During the Great Depression, public sentiment deteriorated regarding women in the workforce. Sadly, workplace discrimination against women experienced resurgence. Women aspiring to have jobs was looked upon as self-serving in a time of economic turmoil. Because jobs were hard to **come by, it was suggested that women should defer to men** instead of competing with them for jobs. After all, employment outside of the home during that time was considered to be an entitlement reserved for men.

Not surprisingly, the pendulum swung in the other direction again when our country entered World War II in the early 1940s. This country's young men were drafted and shipped overseas to defend the U.S. and join forces with Britain, France, and others against the German agenda. During this period, **women were of the mindset that their place was in** the home. But our government needed cheap labor to continue churning out defense weapons, war planes, and the like, in the absence of a substantial segment of the country's young male population. So the media launched a propaganda campaign introducing Rosie the Riveter to the American psyche and lexicon. The purpose of this memorable marketing **campaign was to lure young women back into the workforce** to pick up where male soldiers had left off. Once again, female citizens rose to their nation's challenge by picking up **unfamiliar tools and becoming adept at factory machinery to** support the demands of the defense industry. And for the first time, women also joined the ranks of workers in the fields of government bureaucracy, journalism, etc. "By 1945, 18 million women had joined the American workforce, many **were employed in male-dominated roles like aerodynamics, engineering, railroad workers, streetcar drivers, lumber and** steel mill employees." (U.S. Dept. of Treasury) During that same year, in addition to young, single women, nearly one **out of every four married women worked outside the home** as well.

Sadly, history would repeat itself after the war ended, making it evident once again that a woman's role in the U.S. labor force was dispensable. The men returned home from **the war in the late 1940s and the young women who had stepped up to help their country were quickly ousted from** the workplace. They were either sent back home to the cocoon of domesticity or shuffled off to more traditional "female" occupations like secretary, librarian, waitress, etc. As young women were being released from their occupations in large numbers, soldiers were craving a greater sense of family closeness after witnessing the horrors of the war. American couples started families by the masses leading to a Baby Boom that swept the nation.

But there were other forces at play after World War II as America saw a marked growth in its economy, specifically in the service industry. There had been a marked decline in the birthrate during the Great Depression of the 1930s. This was becoming evident in the make-up of the population which reflected a shortage of adult males by the end of the war two decades later. This shortage of male citizens and workers to cultivate a healthy post-war economy opened up opportunities for a new pool of employable Americans—*working mothers.* In response to the country's need to fill positions in its new service industry, married women with children would join the workforce in large numbers for the first time in American history.

Despite increasing female contributions to the workforce, by the 1960s, the increasing popularity of television resulted in mixed messages. Television programming influenced Americans to believe that married women were still predominantly homemakers. Through post-war propaganda, young *working class* girls were made to believe that the "good life" was defined by achieving housewife status and securing a husband who could be a provider. American employers took full advantage of this publicity agenda and reacted by directing even the gifted college-educated women into "underpaid ancillary positions" until they decided to start a family. Once a female employee chose to start a family, it was not an uncommon practice for these working women to be escorted out the door of their workplace, never to return. However, statistics show that this was not the reality of many women. Against all odds, married women were found to encompass roughly 30-40% of the American workforce during this time.[2]

The sting of women being relegated back into "female" occupations after the short-lived glorification of Rosie the Riveter proved to be too much. The 1960s ushered in a surge of female independence and women's rights groups experienced a revival. Not since the 1920s suffrage movements and **the passage of the 19th amendment had women formed such** a united front; they organized and fought for everything from educational equality to protesting workplace discrimination and unequal pay. This decade would bring about major victories for women's rights in the workplace and in society as a whole. No longer were women going to accept being treated like second-class citizens.

Women could not apply for credit cards in their own name. There had been past reports of women being told, "We don't serve you here," at certain bars and lunch counters. Many similarities could be found between the treatment of women and the treatment of African Americans at this time. It is no surprise that the Women's Rights Movement largely paralleled the Civil Rights Movement for African Americans. In 1963, the Kennedy administration passed the Equal Pay Act which was the first federal law prohibiting sexual discrimination in the workplace (the average female worker's wages were equivalent to 58.9% of the average male worker's earnings).[3] **This law was described as largely**

---

[2] Gail Collins, *When Everything Changed-The Amazing Journey of American Women from 1960 to the Present* (New York: Hachette, 2009) 15.

[3] ibid.,p.105.

symbolic but was an important triumph for women's equality nevertheless. The greatest triumph was not far behind in the form of the Civil Rights Act of 1964. This monumental law was initially put forth by President Kennedy, but after his assassination was signed by President Lyndon B. Johnson. It banned discrimination on the basis of color, race, national origin, religion, or sex. Interestingly enough, the caveat of "sex" as a factor for discrimination was added into that proposal at the last hour but proved to be a substantial victory for the female gender.[4]

Throughout the late 1960s, the U.S. continued to enjoy **a robust economy but the shortage in the adult male population** remained painfully evident. In November 1966, *Time* magazine published an article entitled "A Good Man is Hard to Find So They Hire Women" which blatantly revealed the reliance of the U.S. workforce on female manpower in its time of need.[5] In addition, several large firms targeted stay-at-home moms in recruiting campaigns. Widespread marketing agendas introduced the "two-income" family ideal into the American culture as a tactic to entice stay-at-home moms to join the workforce where they were needed. The "two-income" family was placed at the forefront of the propagandists' agenda. American households were lured into believing that two incomes were essential to afford the necessities that the "good life" had to offer. This era marked an increase **in detached single family homes, second family cars, second televisions, summer camp for kids, washer/dryer combos,** annual family vacations, and college education for the kids.

---

4 Danzinger, op.cit., p.57.

5 Collins, op.cit., p.98.

It's no surprise that when the economy slowed down in the 1970s and 1980s, women's earnings had become a vital component of the family's household income.

Reproductive freedom was realized with the introduction of the birth control pill which gained widespread use by the mid-1960s. This new contraceptive gave women the ability to choose when they wanted to start a family and allowed more time to focus on education and career advancement. Contraception "gave employers more confidence that women would be reliable employees for the long-term and therefore better suited for more permanent positions." College and graduate school enrollments for women soared and women took full advantage of their newfound freedom. Young women began prioritizing higher education and career advancement resulting in the delaying of marriage and child-rearing. The next decade of the 1970s was blemished by the dissolution of many marriages due to a myriad of factors with an unprecedented increase in the national divorce rate. This left women with rising uncertainty regarding their ability to rely solely on a husband for security, wealth, and family stability.[6]

By the 1980s, women's earnings provided a substantial supplement to American household incomes across several sectors of society. The college enrollment statistics for females versus males showed that women valued higher education, not only to achieve a sense of personal fulfillment and purpose, but also to improve their financial station in life.

The average American household of the new millennium has an income profile which shatters the age-old concept of the "sole provider." Households today are primarily

---

6 ibid.,p.102-104.

comprised of "co-providers" and women as higher earners in the marriage is becoming increasingly prevalent for many reasons. Over the past two centuries, women have been extremely successful at obtaining degrees of higher education which leads to greater workforce preparedness. Women have harnessed the power of knowledge to propel themselves from the underclass to a position worthy of equality and respect. Increased intelligence and academic advancement has allowed females to join America's top-earning elite. The ambitions of women to obtain competencies across a breadth of professional fields has earned them a presence in board rooms, surgical suites, and atop courtroom benches.

As the importance of women in the American workforce increases, so does their earning potential. This increased earning potential can alter female ideals for marriage; their definition of a suitable mate; and how they relate to their male counterparts in the workplace and at home. The American marriage as an institution must respond accordingly to rapidly changing ideals or face the possibility of deterioration and dissolution. As a collective, society must navigate carefully yet purposefully around the newest dynamic in American marriages: Female Breadwinners.

Chapter Two
The Perfect Storm

MARRIAGES THAT CONTAIN A FEMALE breadwinner have the potential to rebuke customary gender roles in relationships. Such gender roles were observed in the formative years of most Americans and have served to shape our outlook on life and relationships. According to the National Bureau of Economic Research, in 1975, the majority of American households had a single wage-earner with the husband as the "breadwinner." Several decades ago, traditional roles in marriages were commonplace. Baby-boomers were marrying and starting families at record-shattering rates. They relied on time-honored traditions with regards to the function of husband and wife in the household. The husband's job was to "bring home the bacon" and the wife's job was to cook it up in the pan, take care of the kids, keep the house clean, and look pretty.

In 1987, only 17.8% of wives earned more than their husbands, according to the U.S. Bureau of Labor Statistics.[1] **The nation's periods of economic growth in the 1980s and 1990s had evaporated by the new millennium and in the year 2007,** the nation witnessed the start of the worst recession in recent decades. This recession changed the face of the American labor force through widespread lay-offs and business dis-

---

[1] U.S. Department of Labor, Bureau of Labor Statistics, 1987-2008, Current Population Survey, Annual Social and Economic Supplements, 1988-2009, "Wives Who Earn More than their Husbands" Table 25.

solutions. By 2008, the percentage of wives who out-earned their employed husbands was found to be a startling 26.6%.[2] Although this figure had been rising steadily over decades, the 2007 U.S. recession served to increase conspicuity of such trends in women's incomes.

Such a significant rise in the prevalence of female breadwinners over a 20-year period (1987-2008) can be attributed to several factors acting together synergistically. The two most crucial contributors were female attainment of college education, and an increasing presence of women in the American labor force. When these two factors are combined with the catastrophic effects of the recession, the result can be likened to a perfect storm. This triad of influences pushed females into breadwinner positions in many marriages, and continues to recalibrate the income hierarchy between genders across the nation.

The attainment of college education has probably played the most sustainable role in bolstering women's earnings. Women's incomes are increasingly surpassing their male counterparts. Although women attending institutions of **higher learning feels commonplace in the millennium, this luxury** did not become a reality for most women until long-honored barriers of discrimination were lifted. A report from the National Women's History Museum reveals that it was common practice that "female students were not allowed to take certain courses, participate in certain programs, were restricted **by caps on entrance in certain programs, were held to higher standards for admission, and in some cases not allowed into** particular schools at all."[3] **Luckily, the mid-20th century ush-**

---

[2] ibid.

[3] National Women's History Museum, "A History of Women in Industry" 2007, http://www.nwhm.org/online-exhibits/industry/womenindustry accessed June 2012).

ered in several Supreme Court decisions allowing women the freedom to pursue higher education. The most profound victory, called Title IX, was signed into law by President Richard Nixon in June 1972. This law was an amendment to The Civil Rights Act of 1964, prohibiting sex discrimination in *all* educational programs receiving federal financial assistance. This pivotal legislation would serve to energize the collegiate pursuits of females for decades to come.

After the passage of Title IX, female enrollment into colleges soared. The U.S. Department of Education reports that in 1973, 43% of female high school graduates were enrolled in college; this figure grew to 63% in 1994. Statistics from the National Science Foundation reveal that by 2003 nearly half (49%) of all college graduates in the United States were women. Specifically, women represented 51% of students receiving bachelor's degrees, 53% of those receiving master's degrees.[4] Similar statistics prevail today with women comprising at least half of all college graduates. It goes without saying that once women were allowed a fair shot in the attainment of a college education through legislative support, they took full advantage of these new opportunities for education. Today, the gender underdog has become the majority beneficiary of college education throughout the country.

Another important contributing factor to the recent rise of female breadwinners has been the increasing presence of women in the U.S. workforce. Chapter 1 revealed the history of women in the American workforce which has been tainted by challenges including sex discrimination and a sentiment that work outside the home was an entitlement reserved for

---

[4] National Science Foundation, "2003 College Graduates in the U.S. Workforce: A Profile" Table 4. 2005, http://www.nsf.gov/statistics/infbrief/nsf06304 (accessed May 2012).

the male gender. The largest upstroke in the number of women in the workplace occurred by the end of World War II. This period also saw the greatest activism on the part of women to obtain fair and equal workplace conditions—including attempts to resolve pay inequalities based on gender, lobbying for national health insurance, free daycare for working mothers, and maternity leave.

The female workers of the 1940s served as trailblazers, driving home the sentiment that women were a viable commodity within the country's labor force. Nearly 30 years later in 1969, women comprised 35.3% of the nation's work force. By July 2009, which marked the end of the most recent U.S. Recession, the Center for American Progress reported that women comprised 49.9 % of the country's labor force.[5] **This figure dropped slightly to 49.3 % by February 2012, but remains a true testament to the fact that women's contribution to the workforce serves more than a means to financial gain. Workplace participation also contributes to a modern woman's sense of fulfillment, independence, and personal growth.**

The third and most notable factor increasing the prevalence of female breadwinners in America has been the most recent U.S. Recession. This catastrophic event paralyzed American workers from December 2007 through June 2009. This recession first affected Wall Street and trickled down to Main Street. The financial repercussions of the recession still remain a reality for many Americans today. However, there was one gender who was particularly hard hit by the job loss-

---

5 Maria Shriver and the Center for American Progress, "The Shriver Report-A Woman's Nation Changes Everything," in *The New Breadwinners*, ed. Heather Boushey (Washington: Center for American Progress,2009),33.

es of the recession—the men. This period of economic downturn has therefore been dubbed the "Mancession" because the job sectors that were disproportionately affected were male-dominated fields (i.e. construction, manufacturing, and production)—75% of jobs lost during the recession were experienced by men. They were fired in droves from factories and other blue collar jobs, as well as middle-management positions in corporate America. As a result, many working **women were suddenly thrust into the role of sole wage-earner or "breadwinner" for the entire household. Women who were previously stay-at-home moms and housewives were forced to leave the home in search of work to help support the family through this prolonged period of economic** constraint. Without warning, the number of households with women as top-earners rose exponentially.

While the emergence of female breadwinners may seem like an "overnight phenomenon" to some, a review of women's history regarding education and industry will say otherwise. This perfect storm of females equaling or surpassing **males as college graduates, matching the numbers of males** in the labor force, and sustaining the American family during the most recent Recession has been brewing for decades. The statistics reveal that a new day is on the horizon. "Female breadwinner" now describes roughly 40% of working wives according to 2009 statistics reported by author Liza Mundy.[6]

Breadwinning wives are becoming more commonplace each year. Before long, they will feel more like a normalcy than a taboo.

---

6 Liza Mundy, *The Richer Sex-How the New Majority of Female Breadwinners Is Transforming Sex, Love, and Family* (New York: Simon & Schuster, 2012) 39.

This trend has little chance of reversing itself, or even reaching a plateau any time soon. By assessing some key statistics as predictors of what is to come, the female breadwinner can truly be described as the newest breed of American wife. When we look at future workforce participation, some intellectuals have interpreted employment projections of U.S. Bureau of Labor and Statistics to be in favor of women workers. It has been reported that 10 of the 15 U.S. job categories expected to grow most in the next decade are female-dominated fields including nursing, accounting, and post-secondary teaching.[7] Another valid predictor of the future is, of course, the income trends of the singles population. If we assess the economic trends of single and childless adults ages 22-30 in major metropolitan cities, women out-earn their male counterparts in 39 of the 50 biggest cities according to Reach Advisors.[8]

The educational success of American females combined with the income potential of the female worker has indeed resulted in the perfect storm. Numerous U.S. households will experience the female breadwinner as a reality over the next several decades. The rise of female breadwinners represents the greatest experiment in gender relations since Adam and Eve. How will the American relationship withstand this trend? It is easy to allow fears, questions, and uncertainties about relationships containing a female breadwinner to hang in the air. Instead, I have chosen to embark on a journey toward truth. This book reveals the truth about female breadwinners and what they desperately need from their mates to survive and thrive.

---

[7] Shriver,op.cit.,p.44.

[8] Mundy,op.cit.,p.53.

Chapter Three
The Interviews

"If he would just say, 'I realize you work hard for our family unit so that we can have a better life.' Even if he would just say it one time, that would be enough, but we haven't gotten there yet."

Interview #1: Monica

1) When you entered into this relationship, did you know that you would be earning more? If so, what made you comfortable with that? How did your mate feel about this dynamic?

Not really, I always thought we would make about the same amount. When we first got married he would do whatever it took to take care of the family. But it didn't progress that way. When I first started making a little more, he would say he didn't care as long as when he went to the ATM and the money was there, and our bills are paid, I'm OK with it. That's how it was in the beginning.

There has been more of a problem as the income gap has widened over the years. There has been a slow decline with his attitude. It's an underlying current that manifests itself in other ways in our marriage. I guess it's the control thing as well. So I try to do other things to try not to emasculate him.

2) How does this arrangement with you as the breadwinner make you feel?

I feel a little resentful. I have a full-time job and I have an extra job that I love. I leave in time to drop off and pick our children from school because that is important to me. Then I go home and do stay-at-home Mom stuff, then I work from 7 to 11pm, and he is just enjoying life. He is working, but I feel if I am "hustling" then he should be 'hustling.' He has the ability to earn what I am earning so he should go do it. If I feel that he is spending money frivolously out with his friends, it makes me think, 'Wow... I worked so hard to get that and he is just spending it.' I don't say anything but I just feel kind of resentful about it.

3) Do you feel comfortable with your family and friends knowing that you earn more? Why or why not?

I would say no. I have one good girlfriend that I confide in. I don't really talk about it. I don't want other people to think that he is not taking care of us. I don't want people to think that I am in control, especially in my culture. So I don't volunteer that information. I just don't disclose it. He will make some edgy comments that are negative pertaining to how much I make.

4) What feelings do you hide about this relationship dynamic that you can never tell him?

I feel that he should have a little more of a 'hustle.' He is making a conscious choice to not be a go-getter. He could have more drive. He is content with just being [average]. I see him as being a little bit lazy. That is unattractive to me but I could not tell him that. I don't think I should make all of the financial decisions, but I feel that he should be a little more conscious about how he spends money because even though it's our money, I feel like it's on my back.

I think he has changed over the years. I think maybe it's my fault because I have worked so hard over the years that maybe he has decided that I will handle everything so there is no need for him to push so hard. Maybe I should have stepped down a little bit and let him step up to handle things financially. I wonder if it's my fault that he feels like I will take care of it.

5) What does "head of household" mean to you? Who is the head of the household in your home?

Head of household is the person who sets the tone and the goals and the direction of the family—of the entire unit. It doesn't have so much to do with money. I see myself as the head of the household. I would never tell him that. He probably knows that I think I'm the head and resents it.

6) Would you consider leaving your career behind if it was causing your relationship to suffer?

I have never thought of leaving my career behind. But what I have done which is just as bad is [I refrain from discussing my career with him]. He could not tell you anything about what I do pertaining to my career advancements or much of anything about my job. I just withhold that information. I just don't share my successes with him. He sees making more money as [obtaining more] power and he probably thinks that I think I am running the show because I make more money. But I could be poor and I would still be the same way. It's just my personality.

I realized how much of a problem it was for him when we were playing Scrabble with some other people. In the middle of the game he just stopped playing, got up and left the room and said, 'Just because you have the title you have and make the money you do, doesn't make you smarter than me!' I was shocked because I didn't know he felt that way. He had been keeping it all inside. That was about two years ago. Since that time, I find myself tiptoeing around him, making sure I don't come across [like a know-it-all]. I feel like I have to dumb myself down.

7) What are your overall expectations of a spouse in a relationship? If those expectations have not been met, what do you think has prevented this?

I expect some mutual respect, some collaboration in the decision-making [process]. Not just me making decisions or just him making decisions, but working together to discuss and make decisions. I just want to feel recognized and appreciated. I wish that he could support [me] and be proud of me for what I do for a living. I don't care so much about the money, because I enjoy what I'm doing. But if I felt appreciated, I wouldn't feel so resentful about the money.

8) How similar is your relationship to your parents' relationship? Is that acceptable to you?

In my relationship, I see him becoming more like my father and that is not acceptable to me. My father was the dominant 'alpha male.' My mother was nowhere near the breadwinner. In my parents household it always my father's way or the highway—my father was always in control.

I see my husband trying to take on the dominant role with silly little things like—the car has to be parked in a certain way in the garage and it's got to be that way or the refrigerator has to [be organized] a certain way. I think this is his way of showing me who is 'the man' in the house. He has said to me, 'There is only room for one man in this house—you need to act like the woman.'

I would like for him to take a strong role in the household but not in an aggressive way. I want him to have a direction for the family but in a different way. He seems to resent my input into discussions instead of having some collaboration. He says things like 'you're not always right—it doesn't always have to be your way.' I think it's the money difference.

9) *Why did you get married?*

I got married because culturally we [as women] couldn't move out and live on our own. I met him and he had the right mix of culture and edginess. I thought I would never find that mix again. Looking back I realize he had the same traits then but I just didn't realize it because I was so young. I wanted to get out of the house. We were raised in a very conservative culture: Men run the show and marriage is the only way to go.

My dad said my marriage would not work [from the beginning]. He said I was a high-achiever and he didn't see the same thing in [my husband]. He said my husband was not going to be able to handle me; he told my future husband the same thing. My husband said he didn't care about how much I made; he would be able to handle it. I now understand what my father was talking about.

10) If you have children, what type of individual do you want them to marry? Is it different from your relationship and why?

I would tell my sons not to marry someone if they could be not a provider for them. If they want to marry a high-earner, then they need to be high-achievers also. I would not want them to marry someone who is going to out-earn them. I want them to be able to be the primary wage earner for their household. I want my daughter to be very independent. I want her to go to school but… hmmm, I don't [really] know what I want for her. I also think being a high-wage earner may limit her marriage potential.

11) Do you think that more people are satisfied or dissatisfied with this relationship dynamic and why?

I would say many women in our realm say they would rather live alone than be in that marriage dynamic. We tend to outgrow our partner. When the kids hit a certain age, they just call it quits in the marriage.

Sometimes my husband's friends will make little digs to him about my position and salary. Then I will get the cold shoulder from my husband for a couple of days. I blame him for putting that information out there. I always try to play down my job title/salary.

When I recently told my husband I got a big promotion, my husband just said, 'Oh, ok.' I got no praise or recognition from him, so I called my father thinking [at least] he would be proud of me. He said, 'You have to choose between family and career because a man can only take so much.'

12) Is trust, support, or responsibility a factor in your relationship?

Support is definitely an issue in my marriage. Trust is also an issue. My husband has had an affair with someone who thought he was God's gift. We went to counseling and got over it. He felt that I was always too busy—so he found someone whom he felt appreciated him. However, I do trust him now because I don't think he would do it again.

13) Would you encourage others to have the same relationship dynamic? Why or why not?

I would discourage people from getting into this type of relationship. I would say date somebody who is equal to your income level. Otherwise, it comes back to haunt you later.

14) What advice would you give to other women who may be entering a similar arrangement?

I would consider going old school by putting all of the money into one account. Having separate accounts just makes the income disparity more apparent. It has led to the slow destruction of our marriage. Separating our money has not been good for us. I think it's better for the marriage to put all the money together. Things were better for us when we both had our checks deposited into one account. When you take ownership of the money then you are isolating the money. This is good [only] if your partner is financially responsible.

15) Is there communication between the two of you regarding this topic or is it like the elephant in the room?

We don't talk about it in a nice sort of way. It will usually come out of some kind of problem. He wanted to start a business. I was hesitant but I thought maybe this is [his way] of trying to show initiative. So I said ok. We dumped a lot of money into the business because I wanted to support his business. Eventually, he started letting the business drop and wasn't so serious about it. I called it to his attention and he said he didn't want to do the business anymore because he did not want to hear my comments. He saw it as me trying to run or control the business. Everything I try seems to come back to me in a negative way. So I try to avoid the money conversations. I have told him I don't want to be in charge of everything.

16) Do you feel that more money should equal more voice in the marriage?

No. I don't think it should but I think it does add to more of a voice. It's on my back. The older you get the more tired you are, the more you want to relax, and the more you don't want the responsibility. I don't want to have to do this. I want to be able to take some time off. But I have a lot of financial pressure because of our lifestyle. So if I feel the pressure then I feel I have more power... I am the one who has to say, 'We are not going to spend the money that way.' I never say it's because I made the money so we are going to spend it in a certain way. I always tie it into something else, like we need to save more money for certain things, kid's college, etc. It's a lot of pressure and I don't want the pressure. I know he doesn't perceive it that way. He doesn't understand how I feel.

17) Do you ever feel the need to over-compensate for this difference in income? In what way? How does your mate respond to that gesture or behavior?

This is where I am conflicted. I would like to see traditional marital roles. That's what I would like. It should be a respectful union, I still feel that way. However, I do believe that the man should be the [leading] force in the house. If I didn't believe that I would have been divorced a long time ago. I think the children need that [balance]. I can be the most independent woman, making a million dollars, but children need to see a strong man in their life. I feel my children should see me caring for them and their father making the decisions. [Some may say] that's very antiquated, but I do believe that.

18) How has your current dynamic affected your expectations for your spouse and his "role" in the relationship?

I expect that my husband would not hide things from me. For example, he has been going on job interviews and has never shared that with me. Why would he not share that with me? I expect the same type of support that I expected when we first got married. Do I get it? NO. My needs are not financial.

I'm always trying to find ways to make him feel like he is in control. I'm trying to always involve him in the children's school meetings, etc. I've started asking his permission when it comes to the children's affairs like sleepovers, etc. He seems to appreciate it. Sometimes I think he takes advantage of it. When he makes a decision, if I don't agree with it, then he feels that I should not question his decision. So I try to step back and let him have the final say. I've been trying this approach for about six months now. I'll see if it helps. I don't know if it will help though.

19) What do you need from your mate that you are not getting? What do you think your mate needs from you that he is not getting?

I want someone to share my life with. I would like to be supported. I used to be timid but now I can say I am smart. I would like somebody to say, 'Yes, you are smart and I am proud of you for that.' I just want to be able to be myself and not have to hide my abilities so as not to emasculate him. I have to hide the things about myself that I am most proud of. I just want to be able to be myself.

He needs for me to be more submissive. He wants me to allow him to 'be the man' and make every decision. This makes him feel more masculine and more in charge. I don't do that all the time because I have to work so much. But I have to work all the time to maintain our lifestyle. If I didn't have to work so hard, I would have more time to spend with him. If I were to let some of the work go, our whole lifestyle would be different.

20) What can your mate do to smooth over some of the bumps in the road with regards to the salary difference in your marriage?

He could acknowledge my salary in a positive way and appreciate what I do. If he would just say, "I realize you work hard for our family unit so that we can have a better life." If he would say to me, "Can I support you in any way?" Versus, "I'm resentful and I don't want to be a part of it." Even if he would just say it one time, that would be enough, but we haven't gotten there yet.

Interview #2: Sharon

1) When you entered into this relationship, did you know that you would be earning more? What made you comfortable with that? How did your mate feel about this dynamic? How do you feel about this situation now compared to when you entered the relationship?

I never thought this would be the case. I thought we would complement each other and that we would be able to grow from where we were. If I had known that I would be the breadwinner, I think I still would have gotten into the marriage, but I would have had a different conversation.

A problem comes into play when a man is not honest about what his money situation is. That skews the relationship. I don't mind that you don't make as much money as I do but what else are you going to do to contribute?

That is the conversation that we never had. We went into the relationship thinking, "OK, we both make this amount of money and we are going to be able to afford a nanny or housekeeper," and that is not the case. Since that is not the case, is the husband going to be able to pick up those pieces and help out more? If the husband is not willing to help out more, then that creates an issue. How are we going to make this household work?

2) How does this arrangement with you as the breadwinner make you feel?

It makes me feel good. I don't [view it in a negative way]. However, I did feel a little bit strange because my dad was always the main breadwinner. I was raised that way. Initially, it was really a shock because I never knew anything else. I had this idea of the man as a supporter, but then I realized that society is changing. The traditional roles that we grew up with are not the "end all be all" type of thing.

But at the same time, what is the other person willing to do? Are they willing to switch roles? And that's when we began to have an issue. My thought is, "Okay, you are not doing 'XYZ' so now you have to be doing 'ABC.'" And the other person says I'm not doing "ABC" because that is not my role. Well, if you are not going to be out there working a 9-5, then you have to be doing "ABC" because with one income we cannot afford to hire somebody to come in and do all these things.

3) Do you feel comfortable with your family and friends knowing that you earn more? Why or why not?

I think the embarrassment is not that I earn more. It's the fact that the other person is not doing their part. I'm embarrassed because I have to go out and work a 9-5 and then come home and still do all the traditional things—that's what I'm embarrassed about!

If I had a husband who said I'm not going to work but when you come home, dinner is going to be ready and the house is going to be clean, I would not have a problem with that. But when the husband is out playing golf every day and I still have to come home and cook dinner, wash clothes, and clean the house, that's a problem for me. I still have to do all the traditional roles even though I work a 9-5 job.

My marriage got to the point where my husband said, "I'm only going to have a certain type of job [as an attorney]. If I can't be the head honcho then I will be nothing." I said there is no place for that in this marriage. That's what caused the demise of my marriage—because I think, "If I have to work and come home and do all this stuff, then why do I need you? You are another dependent. You are not adding any value. I resent you because you are not adding any support. You don't want to work. You won't take just any job; you say it has to be only a certain type of job. You don't want to help around the house, so I may as well not be with you. I don't need another dependent."

4) What feelings do you hide about this relationship dynamic that you can never tell him?

I have not hidden anything. I have told him how I feel. I was one who waited later in life to get married. I got married after 35 and had kids later. I got married because I wanted to have kids and a family, and I thought my life would be a certain way and that didn't happen.

I felt that I had sacrificed so much in college. I could have had the convertible car but I was always very practical with my money because I felt that when I had kids I wanted to be able to have a certain lifestyle. I didn't live my life the way I wanted when I was younger and I was very resentful during my marriage. I said, "This is not going to work. You need to participate in this relationship."

I went so far as to say, "You need to have the house clean. You need to have dinner ready and pick up the kids. Do these certain things around the house." He refused to be in that role and it further deteriorated our marriage. I have to cook and clean when I come home. He would say he has things to do. So I felt as if my life was put on hold because I have to come home and do all these things. He thinks he is just supposed to play golf all day?

There were times when I would come home from work and I would have a meeting to go to or I wanted to meet a friend for dinner. He would say he has something else to do and he couldn't watch the kids. I said, "Oh no! This is not going to work!" Eventually, our lifestyle started to deteriorate. It was the lifestyle that I had made and because I could not go any further, that was where we stood. So instead of our lifestyle increasing [over time in our marriage], it actually decreased. I just could not maintain everything I had to do. The house was constantly dirty. I just didn't have enough energy to cook dinner, wash the clothes, and take care of the kids. I just couldn't do it all. Things around the house were starting to break down and my husband would not even get things fixed.

5) What does "head of household" mean to you? Who is the head of your household?

I was head of household. The head of household to me means the person who is most concerned with everything that goes into making the house a home. My husband never had that experience. He previously lived with his parents before he moved into my house. I just think he never knew how to pay the electric bill and realize that there are things that you have to do to maintain a household.

I think he just took things for granted. So it was always me wanting to know, "Is the mortgage paid? Is the gas paid?" He was the fun one. He would say, "Let's go here and do this." He never worried about the substantial things. That's what head of household means to me—the one who takes the ultimate responsibility for running the household.

Head of household makes decisions about what is best for the household. My husband always made selfish decisions. He made decisions based on what was best for him and not for the household. Looking back I think maybe that should have been a red flag, but because he was an attorney, I thought to myself, "How could it be?" Sometimes you discount red flags because you want to be fair. My biological clock was ticking and I wanted to have some kids and be married. I never investigated the full story. I didn't want to turn my nose up because of his less-than-perfect living situation.

6) Would you consider leaving your career behind if it was causing your relationship to suffer?

No! I would never consider leaving my career because I never saw any steady income from him. I would have been scared to put all my eggs in one basket. Over the years of our marriage, he wasn't committed to getting a job to support his family. Even if he never found the "perfect job," he could have been digging ditches or doing whatever it took to take care of his family. He just didn't have that drive.

7) What are your overall expectations of a partner/spouse in a relationship? If those expectations have not been met, what do you think has prevented this?

To me a spouse is someone who truly has your back. It means being "Mr. Mom" if you have to be, or taking a substitute teacher position that you don't really want but you do it anyway if it helps to provide for your family. He should be flexible enough to do whatever he must do for his family, without having pride and ego get in the way.

I think the key is that he wasn't raised that way, over the years he developed a sense of pride that he couldn't let go. I think that to a certain extent he had been living a falsehood for so long that he just had to continue to live out those lies. I think eventually he was feeling like, "I can't be exposed."

I think dishonesty prevented my expectations from being met. In the beginning of our marriage, he presented a picture that his family was well off, having a big house, even describing two Christmas trees for the holidays. When I first visited his family [out of town], I saw that they lived in a rinky-dink house. However, I was too far into the relationship at that point. I thought to myself, this is nothing like what was described. I felt that if I were to leave him because of this superficial reason, I would be the bad person. I didn't think it was right to leave someone because he didn't have the money that [he] led me to believe he had. You make compromises and you make choices in life.

8) How similar is your relationship to your parents' relationship? Is that acceptable to you?

My marriage was not at all like my parents. My parents got married at a time when there was complete honesty. I think that back then, people started out with so very little that it didn't matter. Whereas when I got married I had my own house and I owned an apartment building. Nowadays, you may start off the marriage with you both having a lot, or one person has a lot and the other has a little. When my parents got married they didn't have that much to lose. My parents grew up on a farm and they both just had suitcases of clothes.

So now people are getting married later in life and they have accumulated things. They need to be able to either protect these things or say to themselves that it's not that important to me if I lose them. So I think that's a big part of marriages today. When I got married my mom said, "You've got have something on the side for yourself."

But I wanted to believe in love. I wanted to have complete openness and trust. I did not want to go into the marriage holding back and expecting the worse. I just wanted to jump in completely exposed and trusting. Nowadays, couples are getting married later and it's harder to do that. I did listen to my mom and kept my separate bank account. I did the research and found out that my house is still my house, but in terms of laws I didn't do anything formal like a prenuptial agreement. If I had to do it again, I would do something formal.

9) Why did you get married or enter into a long-term relationship?

I got married because I thought I had found someone whom I could build something with. I got married at a point in my life when I really wanted to have two children and my clock was ticking. I thought I had found someone that I could do that with and we could build something together, someone that I could share my life with. So, I jumped at that opportunity.

10) If you have children, what type of individual do you want them to marry? Is it different from your relationship and why?

I really want my [kids] to marry someone who will sacrifice whatever because sometimes circumstances arise in life. The important thing is that as long as that person can put their pride aside, together they can accomplish anything. If they can just do what's best for the family. You hear stories about superstars who hit rock bottom, but then they were able to rise to the top again.

If a man can let his pride down just enough to do what he needs to do for his family, then that is the magic formula that can propel you to greatness. If he can say, "No matter what is going on, we are going to get through it." It's that attitude that will carry you through the relationship... for women to have their husbands to love them like Jesus loves us. Once you do that, there is nothing that person won't do for you.

11) Do you think that more people are satisfied or dissatisfied with this relationship dynamic and why?

I think that women can be satisfied in this type of relationship—it just depends on the type of husband that they have. To me, it's not about the money; it's about the commitment. What are you going to do to help improve the family? If you are not going to do anything then you are disposable to me.

If you are not valuable by making my life easier and the kids' lives easier, than you are not helping me—you're hurting me. You are a hindrance. The key is that it's about the attitude, the support, and the man's comfort level.

12) Is trust, support, or responsibility a factor in your relationship?

Yes, all of it was. There was no responsibility in terms of what I thought his duties should be. There was no trust because I had no idea what he was doing during the day. My husband knew that I was resentful about him going out having lunches and playing golf during the day. He just started lying about what he was doing. So I said to him, "Now you are lying about stuff."

It just compounded the situation. I was resentful when he told me the truth, but it was even worse when he started lying.

I think that my husband was coddled by his parents. We are in the middle of a divorce now and his father has the ultimate authority on visitation with the children. His father has not yet recognized who his son is. I told my father-in-law that my husband is not on time to pick up his children—or to drop them off. These are the visitation times that my husband chose, not me. Yet, he can't even be punctual with his own times that he put forth. I told his father that these times have to be convenient for both of us. I have things planned in my life and so you guys can't just switch up the script. His father refuses to see what his son is doing wrong.

13) Would you encourage others to have the same relationship dynamic? Why or why not?

I wouldn't encourage women to get into this type of relationship. It just makes things harder. But that's not the answer—I think it depends on the attitude. If I was a "kept" woman and could just be at home, I would still have strong feelings about that! You need to talk about things before you get married. If you want to be a stay-at-home mom, then do that. If you want to be in the workforce, then do that. There needs to be a happy balance. You need to find your own happiness.

14) What advice would you give to other women who may be entering a similar arrangement?

Observe your intended husband in different social settings. Is he ashamed to say what his job is? How does he act around your family? What else is he doing to help support you other than finances?

15) Is there communication or is this topic like 'the elephant in the room'?

Yes, we talked, but his actions were not congruent with the conversation. His point of view was always, "Don't you think I feel bad enough about not having a job?" My response was, "Okay, I understand that, but why are you turning down these jobs?" Opportunities came but they were not prestigious enough for him so he refused the opportunities. So, I can only look at the actions and not just the conversations. He didn't have a job for over four years, so we had to talk about it.

16) Do you feel that more money should equal more voice in the marriage?

I don't think the woman has to have more of a voice if she earns more. Conversation should be what's best for the family. If you are doing what's best for the family then it's not an issue. Things need to be discussed such as playing golf every week or going to the hair salon every week. Neither one of those things should be discounted if you can afford it. But, at the same time, there needs to be equality in terms of responsibility, but what are you doing to support the other person?

17) How has your current dynamic affected your expectations for your spouse and his "role" in the relationship?

I expected his role to change. That was really the issue. When we first got married, I thought he was going to be the breadwinner. I thought my income was going to be secondary and supplementary. I thought his role would change, and when it didn't, that's when all hell broke loose. He said, "I'm not going be Mr. Mom and I'm not going do these things." That was unacceptable to me.

18) What do you think your mate needs from you that he is not getting?

I don't know what he needed from me that I didn't give. For four years I tried to be the understanding wife. I would get close to the breaking point. But I was always hoping that if he could get just that great job, then everything would be okay. Then I realized that the job was not really the problem, it was the lack of support. It was the lack of the mentality to sacrifice. I eventually got to the point when I realized that even if he could have gotten that fabulous job, I would still feel like "peace be with you." It was not going to change anything.

I've talked to my sister and my mom about the dynamics of the relationship over the years. They have had the opportunity to observe. They say that I have done everything that I could have done. I feel confident about getting this divorce. I have given him the 2nd, 3rd, 4th, and the 10th chance for him to change. I was in limbo for over four years! I feel like I've done everything. I don't know if he would agree. But the kids and other things must be considered, too. People reassured me that I have done the right thing. People tell me, "How did you stay married as long as you did?"

19) What do you need from your mate that you are not getting?

He didn't give me his all. I really went into the marriage thinking about our religious ceremony—that said that your husband should love you as Jesus loved us. I really expected that he would do anything to keep the family afloat. I never thought his pride and ego would lead to the demise of this marriage; I didn't think that his ego would come before the family. I wasn't raised that way. I have worked at McDonalds before. I have done a lot of things in my life and I just wasn't raised in that type of environment. I look back and I think that he loved me as best as he could—but just not the way I needed to be loved. My love is about sacrifice and his love is about, "As long as I don't have to do XYZ."

We hit a point when it could no longer be the way that he wanted. It had to be about what is necessary for the family. We have been married [for] years.

I think at a point in the beginning, him getting the right job could have saved things. Then his selfish attitude would not have been so exposed. He is who he is and the real person will come out when placed in certain situations. As long as he had that comfortable job, that other side of him probably would not have been exposed. His selfish decisions would not have been exposed as long as he had the money to pay for the selfish decisions. But when he didn't have the money, he still wanted to make the same selfish decisions.

Interview #3: Melissa

1) *When you entered into this relationship, did you know that you would be earning more? What made you comfortable with that? How did your mate feel about this dynamic? How do you feel about this situation now compared to when you entered the relationship?*

No, I didn't know that I would be the main breadwinner. When we met, I was still in graduate school and my mate had been working in corporate America for 10 years. He had built financial wealth by the time we got married. I guess he was comfortable with the dynamic, knowing that I had the potential to increase my earning potential over time. I was getting my Masters [degree] when we met.

I have mixed feelings about the situation now. Sometimes it's ok and [there are] times when it's not ok. I have thoughts that the male should be the main breadwinner in the family and should be able to provide financial support and stability in the family.

On the flip side, I am an independent woman. I made the decision to go to college and get my Master's degree and have my own career to create stability on my end. So I'm not depending on a man as a provider/decision maker. My husband is very confident and self-assured, so he's not bothered by the fact that I make more. At least that's the impression I get.

2) *How does this arrangement with you as the breadwinner make you feel?*

It's that mixed emotion that I mentioned before. For the most part all is well with us, because I have a husband who's very confident in [who he is] as a man. He doesn't see his success or contribution or value only based on his income. He's very supportive of me in my career. He's not trying to hold me back. He's moved several times as my career has grown over the years.

But there are times when, you know, having children, I wish I could stay at home or work part time. My husband could have a job earning a lot more than me. He's just making a choice to do what he's doing now. He has a skill set to earn much more. So I get frustrated because I want to be able to spend more time with the children. I would like to work part time or [maybe] take time off from work—maybe one or two years—knowing that I can go back into the work force in a couple of years. But when that conversation comes up, it's almost not entertained because he doesn't want to go back to the corporate environment.

3) Do you feel comfortable with your family and friends knowing that you earn more? Why or why not?

It doesn't matter, but it's not something that we talk about. With my circle of friends, we don't talk about how much I make or how much he makes. It has not been an issue with us. He has not expressed any embarrassment or shame about the situation. I'm a little indifferent with that question. If I knew he was uncomfortable, it would never come up in conversation. We have a mutual respect and admiration for each other, so I would never do anything to let him feel less of a man.

4) What feelings do you hide about this relationship dynamic that you can never tell him?

Sometimes, what seeps into my mind are those stereotypical thoughts about how we have traditionally defined the role of a man and the role of a woman. I may be having a very difficult week at work and he [may be] on the road traveling for work. I'm at home taking care of the kids alone and thinking that I wish things could be different. What would life be like if things were different? I wish he would do more: be the man, bring in more income, so there's a little bit more balance. I do feel like I am carrying the financial weight as well as being the primary care-taker, and having to balance it all. Therefore, there are times when I feel resentment towards the situation. But whenever I get those feelings, it's because mentally I may not [be] in a happy place due to the stresses of trying to handle it all.

If we have a conversation about that, I would probably beat around the bush a bit. I would say, "Why don't you go back to corporate? You could have a VP job. You still have flexibility, do something that you know you can do." It is not directly saying, "You need to go get a job." I'm doing something that I know I can do. Would I want to do this all the time? NO. I feel like I'm making sacrifices for the family and I just don't see that from him.

5) What does "head of household" mean to you? Who is the head of the household in your home?

We don't talk about head of household. We have more of a partnership. We view ourselves as equal partners in our marriage and in our relationship, in terms of raising our family. But we also recognize [that] as a mother, I play a different role when it comes to the kids. And as a wife, I play a [separate] role; and for him, he plays a different role as a father.

We draw from each other's strengths. It's not so much that we define things that we do as a man's job or a woman's job. I enjoy cooking so I make meals for my family. We make decisions as a couple, unless I'm being a renegade.

6) Would you consider leaving your career behind if it was causing your relationship to suffer?

Hell NO! I would not dumb down my income or slow track my career for him. Nor do I think he would want me to do that. If my relationship were suffering, then we would need to figure out why and how we work together to resolve it. However, [I would consider that] if it were an inconvenience for my family, because the higher up I go, the more responsibility and accountability I have. [If] my job required me to be away from my family, or a promotion stopped me from having quality time with my family, then I would probably turn down that promotion.

7) What are your overall expectations of a partner/spouse in a relationship? If those expectations have not been met, what do you think has prevented this?

My expectation of a partner in a relationship is somebody who is going to provide love, [a] safe environment for me and for the kids, [someone who] is going to respect me as a woman, and as a mom. My expectation is also that my spouse will provide financial support for the family—financial support that provides the basic necessities. Anything above that is great, because we are not the type of people who want to keep up with the Jones' or live above our means or run up credit cards and pay the minimum month to month. I don't have high expectations when it comes to the finances, but at the same time, I expect that he would provide a level of financial support now and in the future.

I think in the beginning of a marriage we are getting to know and understand each other—our differences, what makes us click. Like respect, for example, respect is very important to me. What it means to me is something very different than what it means to my husband-which I can't understand. I think part of it is cultural. He had to learn what respect means to me and I had to learn that respect is not that high on his list. Honesty is higher on his list.

But it was more in the beginning of our marriage. I [was not born in the U.S.]; but he [was]. People think because we [both live in America] that we culturally share the same views, but I have very strong cultural ties that are different, and it doesn't mean that I wanted to offend him or hurt his feelings.

For example, in [my country] we invite folks over to our house and we will eat and drink and there are no expectations that the person would need to chip anything in—you don't have to bring anything. One of the things I've learned is that the whole ["going Dutch" thing]-he was comfortable with [that]. I'll put my credit card out and will pay for everyone's dinner, because

I know next month I [will] go with my friends and they will do the same. But he doesn't feel that way. I think he has adjusted over the years, which is good to see.

It makes me crazy that family members think that our lifestyle is provided by my husband. 'Look what her husband has provided for her,' when actually I am the one who does most of the providing. It usually happens with people who are older. They seem to assume that the husband is doing the providing. I have an expectation that he will make the correction. I would like to have recognition. I don't need to be stroked but don't put me down either.

8) How similar is your relationship to your parents' relationship? Is that acceptable to you?

My dad is very financially stable. My parents are not together. My dad's wife has always worked and contributed. He is clearly the man of the house, even if she has her own thoughts and ideas. She is more submissive. They don't have the same level of equality that there is in my marriage.

My mom is not as financially secure as us, but she wants to focus on other things rather than where she is, financially, today. In my childhood, I saw the woman play more of a submissive role. I don't look at any of them as role models. I've seen relationships where the woman stayed in the relationship longer than she wanted to because she didn't have the income to go out on her own. She was very much dependent on her husband for everything. She didn't have much of a voice in her marriage. I've always been a very independent person. I knew that I had a voice and that drove me to find a partner who could value that. [I didn't want someone who] felt like he could control my every move and make all the decisions and feel like I'm not going to provide my input.

I think my income allows me to have more of a voice. I knew I didn't want to be submissive to anyone. So, I needed a partner to respect that. My income and education allows a level of comfort and stability, and if he feels offended and wants to leave, then go. I guess a part of it is ego. Especially if someone is trying to take you for granted or trying to have control over you as a human being.

9) Why did you get married or enter into a long-term relationship?

I fell in love with this person. I wanted to have children. I wanted the companionship and friendship. I wanted to spend the rest of my life with this person to show my level of commitment. [I wanted to] build a future with [him]. We have a beautiful family and our life is filled with love and laughter.

10) If you have children, what type of individual do you want them to marry? Is it different from your relationship and why?

I never really gave a lot of thought to that. I still have a ways to go before my children are at the age of marital consent. But because my husband and I are both educated individuals with very strong home values, I would want that for them. Somebody who is going to love them, respect them, respect us as their parents, and honor them. It doesn't matter about the race or if one of them is gay, as long as the mate will take good care of them. [Someone] who shares similar values when it comes to education, and just continues [to grow]. If [my daughter] decides she doesn't want to go to college and goes into the arts, we know we have raised a beautiful daughter. I wouldn't want someone to not want to marry her because she decided she wanted to be a ballerina.

So, I would not want to place that kind of pressure on her if they both have that drive and stability. I have friends where both of them make a whole lot of money, but they are not happy. So at the end of the day, I try to teach [my children] that happiness does not come from material things. I don't want them to have to think they have to date someone in a certain financial category.

11) Do you think that more people are satisfied or dissatisfied with this relationship dynamic and why?

Most of the couples that I saw, I think the wives made more, but it never really came up in conversation. So, I don't know if there was a level of dissatisfaction. I tend to think that in today's day and age, this is becoming more of a concern as more women are entering the work environment, going to college, securing degrees, having great jobs, and even making more than their partners.

12) Is trust, support, or responsibility a factor in your relationship?

Trust is not an issue. Sometimes support comes up. My husband is on the road a lot. I feel like I'm carrying a lot of weight here. I feel that things would [be] different if he made a different choice in his career. But when he is home, [he gets] up in the morning with me. He is very active with taking care of the kids, making breakfast, packing lunch, etc.

13) Would you encourage others to have the same relationship dynamic? Why or why not?

I would not discourage someone from getting into that type of relationship. If you love someone and there is open communication and respect, then I can't make a decision based on whether this person makes more than me. You will probably never be happy. But the important thing is, are there other things there that will sustain the relationship? I think if it's a huge financial gap between [the] incomes, the wider the gap, the bigger the issues. If my husband is making $30,000 and wants to travel and be on the road all the time, there would be a big issue. If the gap is not that wide, it's not that big a deal. For me the income gap is small to moderate.

14) What advice would you give to other women who may be entering a similar arrangement?

My advice is: Know what your foundational values are and stay true to those values. People need to communicate—just lay stuff on the table, talk it through. Flip it a little bit. For many years, men have been making more money, but who is to say that the man has to be the one that is making the most? Just keep the lines of communication open. Make sure you have the foundational values in addition to the financial peace.

15) Is there communication within your marriage or is this topic like the elephant in the room?

Our salary differences are more of an elephant in the room. I think it's because the gap is not that big. We really don't talk about it, but we should. For the most part things are good. Occasionally, I go to that unhappy place because I am not only the breadwinner, but also the primary care giver. I feel like I'm carrying a heavy load. I think if we talked about it and had more of an understanding, then maybe I would not harbor those feelings and I would understand how he is feeling also.

It could be that he says, "For the first couple of years I made more and I contributed more." I don't know because we don't talk about it. If you don't talk about it, there may be something that's there that [is unknown]. I would be in favor of talking it through, but it's so sensitive. What is the right way to talk about it? I don't know.

Here is a scenario. My husband handles the finances. We have a joint checking account and savings account and I have a separate savings account. What drives me crazy is when he is asking me, "What are you spending all this for?" I feel like I worked for this! I would get defensive about his line of questions, when all he's trying to do is manage our finances and balance the books. So, when you don't talk about things and get clarity, you [may] harbor some underlying feelings. They [can] play out in a way that's not productive.

Interview #4: Cicely

1) When you entered into this relationship, did you know that you would be earning more? What made you comfortable with that? How did your mate feel about this dynamic? How do you feel about this situation now compared to when you entered the relationship?

When I entered the relationship, I knew I was making more—only maybe $20,000 more or $25,000 more. Subsequently my husband got another job. Then he got another job where we were making pretty equal amounts but he was able to make overtime so he was making a little bit more. But it was still kind of close. So, if he made $100,000, I might have made $95,000.

Now my husband doesn't work. He was laid off in 2009. He didn't do anything for a while. He said, "I want to see if I can make it without having to go back to a formal job." So, I said, "These are what our bills are so, whatever you are doing, this is the contribution you have to make to the joint account. So, whatever you are doing, if you can put in that contribution, then I'm fine with that." The stipulation I had was I didn't want to be left alone having to be like a single parent. My job is pretty hectic. So, I didn't want to have him off doing whatever.

So, now he [has a side job where he works on commission], he puts in the account what he has to. It's not a whole lot more. One of the things that makes me OK with it. We built everything based on one income, so knowing there was an income disparity, we based the bills on percentage of income. We split the bills based on income. If you make 75% of the income, you pay 75% of the bills; the other person contributes 25%.

We made it so everybody felt they were contributing and nobody felt overextended. This way nobody goes broke. He doesn't care about the income disparity. In his mind he wants to be able to do what he wants to do, and if he still can make his contribution pursuing what he wants, then he's fine with it.

The problem is he [works on commission], and some weeks he doesn't make as much, so the weight falls on me. However, since everything is based on one income, if he comes up short, we are not struggling, but it cuts into my personal funds. So, we've had to cut back, but I agreed to it upfront so I knew it was not always going to work out. He has said, "Do you want me to get a job?" And I know that is going to make him unhappy so the relationship is not going to be better. I say, "Well, this is just a temporary thing, so we will just work through this." Sometimes I feel like, "What if I don't have it? You just depend on me. What happens when my week doesn't work out?" So far it's been like OK. We are just gonna have to work through it.

2) How does this arrangement with you as the breadwinner make you feel?

I think I have periods of resentment more stemming from the fact that I believe he depends on me if things fall through for him. I don't feel like I can depend on him if the tables are turned. But, I'm not walking around resentful. I feel like, "What would happen if I didn't have it? What is your plan to set some stuff aside or to earn more money?" One time he said I save too much, and I said, "What do you think would happen if I didn't have it put aside?" He doesn't say that anymore. Sometimes the relationship has its moments, but I went into this knowing I was the breadwinner so it's not like I'm saying, "What happened?" I know I'm the only one earning any money around here, but I really want him to be happy.

3) Do you feel comfortable with your family and friends knowing that you earn more? Why or why not?

My family and friends know he doesn't have a job. I feel comfortable as long as he feels comfortable. People think he makes a lot more than he does because they see us doing all these things. Normally what I will do—and even though we have this arrangement, to be fair to him, because he is a man and everybody doesn't always look at it like that—what I will do is give him my credit card to run a tab or give him the money so he can pay.

I don't feel like I'm embarrassed about it. I don't feel like I have to hide it from people but know that other people don't always buy into our arrangement. Rather than create a lot of jabber jaw about it, which creates its own issues, I just try to avoid putting it out there. But our close friends and family pretty much know our situation.

4) What feelings do you hide about this relationship dynamic that you can never tell him?

I don't think I hide too much. But the things that annoy me are—and I do tell him—I know he's not open to hearing this because I see him bristle when I bring it up, but he pays child support for [his kids], and when [his kids' mom] calls and says she needs more money, I say, "Where is that coming from?"

In all honesty, [they] are our kids, and I realize that, but you are already paying her additional money and you have to add a certain amount into our household, so when she calls and says she needs more, especially when she has not talked to you about it to agree to it, I'm not feeling it. She doesn't run my household; she doesn't spend my money. Up until three weeks ago, we had three cars, and so I think she thinks we have money.

The [kids] went to private school and I said that was her decision. So, you are not buying anything, but clothes, uniforms, stuff they would normally need to go to school. We are not buying books; we're not paying this or that because that's taking money out of our household. She cannot make a decision on her own and expect us to pay for it. When the other two need something, where's that coming from? She's not paying for my kids, but I'm paying 50% for her kids.

I feel like we do our part and still give her more money. So I've had those conversations with him. He says it ain't no big deal. I'll give him $100. So, I feel like if I give you $100 this time, then she's gonna want $200 next time. So, I get him to try to understand how women think, and how things can snowball—what you give is child support. I understand that he doesn't want the kids to think it's a bad arrangement, but sometimes you have to say, "Honey, we can't do that right now."

I think it's him spending more money when he's not making more money. Now I'm paying his child support. The other piece for me that's hard is I don't ever want [his kids] to feel like my kids get more than they get. How do you balance that without having a free for all?

5) What does "head of household" mean to you? Who is the head of the household in your home?

We've had this conversation at church. I don't think we are there yet. But the concept I can most agree with is [that] the head of household is like the CEO of the company. They may not bring in the most finances, but they make the final decisions. So part of the feedback I've been getting is regardless of the money my husband makes, he is a man. A man needs to be in control of his household, and therefore means that you need to have joint discussions but in some cases, he should be able to make some final decisions. But he needs to share his thoughts for getting to that final decision.

That's hard for me because I feel the person making the most money is in charge of the household. To be fair, we try to live the biblical principles, and one of those is that the husband should be the head of the household. At the same time, the biblical principles don't just stop there, because he should be running the household accordingly. That's why I say we are not quite there.

I agree with that in principle: that you should allow your husband to be in charge of the household. Ultimately, the children should see that. The children don't know where the money comes from, and so if he's not in charge of the household—in word and deed and action—then what's his place?

6) Would you consider leaving your career behind if it was causing your relationship to suffer?

What I have said: "I could be a stay-at-home mom if you could provide the same lifestyle I am used to, then I could stay at home." I went to college, got my Masters to live a certain lifestyle. If you can maintain that lifestyle, then I'm good, but I'm not raising my kids in a subpar lifestyle. I'm not eating beans and hot dogs. I'm not shopping in the dollar store.

7) What are your overall expectations of a partner/spouse in a relationship? If those expectations have not been met, what do you think has prevented this?

A spouse is supposed to be your balance. Where you are weak, they have to be strong. He is a good researcher; I am a better negotiator. He will present me with a paper; I will go negotiate. A good spouse needs to realize their strengths, to help make decisions and support you in those decisions. I think you always have to play fair. Is this the best thing for me and my family? If you can say those things as spouse, then you are meeting those expectations.

My expectations have been met. I didn't go into marriage with unrealistic expectations. I had basic expectations. I don't want to be a single parent. I want to have children; I want you to do right by the children whether we are together or not together. I want you to have an active part in the children's lives. I think love is overrated. When the love dies down, could you stand the other person if you didn't love them? Do you like them as a person? I like hanging out with him. In my darkest days, it's him that I still want to comfort me.

8) How similar is your relationship to your parents' relationship? Is that acceptable to you?

In my parents' household, I think my mother was the primarily breadwinner. There were a lot of similarities between my father and my husband. My mother was the one 99% of the time paying the bills making sure that everything was taken care of. My father was like, "I put the money in the bank; you pay the bills." He didn't have a good sense of how things were. He wasn't good at paying bills.

My husband is very similar. He is the baby of his family. I am the oldest. Maybe being the oldest had something to do with it—he is less fiscally responsible than I am. But my husband is much more involved with the kids and the family—something my father did not do. So, his lack of earning power is not as important to me as him being a good father.

9) Why did you get married or enter into a long-term relationship?

I got married because I knew I wanted somebody to spend the rest of my life with. Somebody I wanted to be with when the kids were grown and gone. Somebody I really liked. When I got married, I wanted to be with someone who was the perfect man for me. He doesn't fuss about stuff that is not significant but he's not a pushover either.

Previously, I was in relationships [where] I felt like I could say or do whatever and never got any pushback. He challenges me intellectually. I feel like he is my intellectual equal. He stimulates me in a lot of different ways. I feel like if we can really sit down and talk about it, we can accomplish anything.

10) If you have children, what type of individual do you want them to marry? Is it different from your relationship and why?

I think it would depend on that child's personality. If I have a needy daughter, I would think maybe she couldn't handle that level of responsibility, but if I had a pretty independent daughter, I would say marry the person who makes you happy—that you love and care about—and cares about you, and will do right by you with what they have. If the husband is lazy and just doesn't want to work, that's different. But, if the husband makes less money, but he's doing what makes him happy, and you make a lot more money, then so what—go for it.

11) Do you think that more people are satisfied or dissatisfied with this relationship dynamic and why?

I think if the man has a weak mind, he's gonna be dissatisfied, because he's gonna listen to his friends or his mother, and your father, who may be telling you about how it should be, but if you have a strong independent mind, and you know it's working for you and you go with it, then you'll be fine. But if you are weak minded, you will find that the very things that people are telling you will manifest into your relationship. I think, though, that a lot of men would not be happy with that arrangement.

12) Is trust, support, or responsibility a factor in your relationship?

Yes, in some cases, because when it comes to finances my husband doesn't like to be questioned about how he is spending the money. Because he feels like, "Well, you have a separate account and I don't question you about that." But I say, "I'm putting my expected amount of money into our joint account, so what's left over is mine, so I'm doing what I'm supposed to do, and you are taking extra money out of the joint account." The issue comes when you are taking out of the joint account. Since I know he's not fiscally responsible, I feel the need to let him know that I'm looking at what he's doing because I need to know that there is enough money to cover what's coming out in the automatic drafts. And if $100 is missing, I want to know why, and he says, "Well, remember that time when . . ." I feel like he needs to let me know that the money needed is not in the account, but he doesn't like to be questioned.

So, recognizing that it's a man thing—we have to talk about it—I don't feel like he's about to run off with all the money, but he just doesn't look at the money in the account before he uses it. We had a repossession of a truck and I had to pay [several thousand dollars] to get our truck out, the car is in my name and I don't want that repossession on my credit, in my name, and I had just gotten a bonus. So, I had to use the whole bonus check to get it out. "If I had not gotten a bonus then, what [were] you doing to come up with the money?"

13) Would you encourage others to have the same relationship dynamic? Why or why not?

People need to start pulling credit reports. Marriages are a business arrangement. You may be in love, but it is a business arrangement. If people are not responsible with their money, then they are not going to be responsible with your money. If your credit score is 500 and mine is 700, then we are not having a joint account.

14) What advice would you give to other women who may be entering a similar arrangement?

If you [have] a history of fiscal irresponsibility, you need to be with someone who is fiscally responsible, and you need to recognize that money management is your shortcoming. You don't need to be the money manager. It's not about being the man or the woman. Whoever is best at it, handles the money. It doesn't mean, "I don't love you," but you just don't write the checks. I wouldn't say don't marry the person. So, I think you have to go into it eyes wide open, maybe meet with a financial planner to work out your finances.

15) Is there communication within your marriage or is this topic like the elephant in the room?

We just went to a marriage counselor. We talked about the disparity between the incomes. He seemed to be fine with it.

We talk about, not much the disparity, but we do talk about him putting in his share.

16) Does making more money equate to having more of a voice in the relationship?

No, I don't think more money equals more of a voice. I could be a stay-at-home mom, but I still have the same voice. There should be equal voices in a marriage.

17) Do you ever feel the need to overcompensate for your earning more?

I sometimes will give him money or my credit card before we leave the house to go out.

18) What do you need from your mate that you are not getting?

I make more money. I have larger expectations at work. I should not have to come home and cook or wash clothes. If we are both working equal work days, then granted its equal. Though we don't make the same money but we are both out of the house all day working. But if you have more flexibility in your schedule then you should say, "My mate is out of here early in the morning. Let me go ahead and fix dinner for him or her," so your mate doesn't look at you like, "What the *%$&! are you doing? What have you been doing all day?"

Then when they come home, there should be no dishes. House should not be a wreck. The energy that could have been spent between husband and wife at night time has been spent with the breadwinner having to do additional duties like cooking, cleaning, etc., so then the woman is tired.

I need recognition that making decisions, coaching people, etc., at my job is mentally taxing. My husband doesn't think I have a challenging job. I would like a level of support that recognizes not only what I do professionally, but by me doing that, I can make a financial contribution to this household. Because I am in a leadership position, I need to be there earlier than the average worker. I need more support for my job.

19) What do you think your mates needs from you?

I think he wants support for his business ventures. He doesn't think that I think the things that he does are important or add value to the family. And I don't. He is putting in all this time trying to build a business and we don't see any money. So, I try to support him to a point, but I think we need to see some money from his business ventures. What's the cost benefit of your business? He probably thinks I need to be more supportive of his businesses.

20) What can your mate do to smooth over some of the bumps in the road with regards to salary differences?

He needs to be more transparent with his income. I don't know when he's putting a check in the bank for our joint account or how much it is for. He works on commission, so I don't know how much [he] needs to work in order for him to make his weekly financial contribution. He'll wait until the last minute and then say he has to work more to meet his contribution. I don't know exactly what he is going to put into the account. I wish he would let me know his schedule and his monetary contribution. Because when he is absent unexpectedly, his household chores fall on me.

Interview #5: Brenda

1) When you entered into this relationship, did you know that you would be earning more? What made you comfortable with that? How did your mate feel about this dynamic? How do you feel about this situation now compared to when you entered the relationship?

No, when we were first married, we made equal amounts. After about three years, my salary started to outpace his. But he had his contract work, so it wasn't that much difference. Then I had the opportunity to do some work for the federal government—I had a salary increase of about 20% over about 10 months. That was a huge jump.

It wasn't an issue at first, but then my work responsibilities increased. My schedule was crazy, yet I was still having to do all the wifely things with the kids, socks and daycare —it became a bit of an issue. At about that time, he wanted to quit his regular salary job—we agreed—and he did contract work full time.

That really put a strain on our marriage because his salary was irregular and yet he was not doing the home things with the kids and all. That was a really huge issue for us. We had a struggle for about 6 months to a year—I think our marriage suffered with me being the major earner in the family and him not and still being the head of the household.

I think it's still very difficult for him. If you take our salary jobs only, I make three times more than him. It's hard for him because, at times, he feels like he's the man of the house and I should be bringing in more money. We have conversations about six to eight months, and talk about the issues or he would drive both of us crazy. He says, "Oh, you want that because you make this amount." There are times when he's frustrated. He feels like he is not living up to his end of the bargain. Those are his words—not mine.

But I think he's OK with it because he manages the house money. We have a house account. It's not his money or my money—and I get an allowance and he gets an allowance. We put all our money into that account and that makes him feel better. It's not like I'm saying, "Here's $5 for you and I'm keeping $25 for myself."

Probably if this dynamic were present at the beginning of our relationship, if I had been an established professional and he was making less, I probably would not have pursued the relationship. It sounds shallow, but it's true.

2) How does this arrangement with you as the breadwinner make you feel?

I'm proud of the fact that I'm able to support our family and that I have achieved what I have in my career, but I don't equate it as being better than or more than him in our relationship. I'm just happy that we are able to provide for our family in a way that we envision.

3) Do you feel comfortable with your family and friends knowing that you earn more? Why or why not?

I don't think it's something most people talk about. As a man, I think most men think that he should be the breadwinner. He will bring it up quicker than I will. It has not been a conscious decision to hide it from anyone. My family knows—and they say they don't expect anything less from me—because I am so driven. His family may or may not know. His family may have a problem with it because they are a little more controlling and nosey, in my opinion. I don't care that my family knows and he doesn't care that my family knows.

4) What feelings do you hide about this relationship dynamic that you can never tell him?

I probably hide when I'm frustrated about household stuff. I can't share with him that I feel that if we were in a traditional marriage and he was the breadwinner, then I would be expected to do the household stuff like grocery shopping, laundry, clean the toilet, [make sure] everybody had clean socks, etc.

But with the role reversal, I can't get him to understand my expecting him to pick up the slack in those areas. So, I just chuck it up and do the wife roles that he could help out with. He has taken on the laundry role—he's been doing that for about two years, but I still do some because he's not efficient at it. But I can't say to him, "If you made X amount then we could do this." I think that would be detrimental to our marriage. I don't think it would ever recover because that would make him feel that, I think, he is less of a man because he makes less.

5) What does "head of household" mean to you? Who is the head of the household in your home?

Head of household is the person that we turn to make the ultimate decisions in our house. For us, he leads and guides us in terms of our spiritual life and worshipping. I expect him to take the lead in setting a positive example for the children. My husband is the head of the household. I don't like every final decision—it has to be something I can live with—but ultimately, he has the final decision in most things. We are going to talk about it and discuss it, but as head of the household, I respect him for that role.

6) Would you consider leaving your career behind if it was causing your relationship to suffer?

We couldn't afford for me to just walk away. I don't know. I can't say no and I can't say yes. I would love to be a stay-at-home mom. I will say I have turned down jobs because of the work and travel schedule and how it would affect my family. I would not stop working just for his ego though. I would not struggle for your ego.

7) What are your overall expectations of a partner/spouse in a relationship? If those expectations have not been met, what do you think has prevented this?

I expect him to consider my feelings. I expect him to continue to treat me the way he did when he got me. I expect open lines of communication even if it makes you feel uncomfortable. I expect him to put me first. I should be second only to God. If you fill all that, the other stuff falls in line.

I think they have been met or we would not have been together for [so long].

8) How similar is your relationship to your parents' relationship? Is that acceptable to you?

My marriage is not all like my parents. My mom was a single mom. I saw her struggle to do whatever it took to make ends meet. She would have given up everything to make her ex-husband happy. He was not my dad. Her marriage was not an equal relationship. She did everything to please him. That prevents me from saying that I will just do anything to make my husband happy. You have to be equals.

My husband's dad was the major breadwinner. He was a business owner. My husband was used to being in a more traditional family—where the husband was the head of the family—in that he was the breadwinner and making the financial decisions, which I think is why it was harder for him in the beginning.

9) Why did you get married or enter into a long-term relationship?

I got married because I was crazy and in love and thought that was what you do. I never thought I would marry young. I had just finished college. When he proposed, I wasn't looking for a ring. I knew we would be together, but I wasn't looking to get married just yet. I loved him, so I said yes when he proposed. We were graduating college, so I knew financially we would be fine.

10) If you have children, what type of individual do you want them to marry? Is it different from your relationship and why?

I don't care financially what [they make]. I think from a social perspective and education exposure and experience, they should be equal... but I see in one of [them] would not be able to handle it. He would be competing with his wife the whole time. The other [child] would not care. He would not care if he made $1 and she made a million. They know that I make more than Dad. We don't hide that fact in our household.

Some of my friends have men who start off saying they can handle it—you can see a shift in the relationship as he realizes that, no, he can't handle it when she can go out and buy herself a BMW and he can't buy her the rims to go on it. I have heard women complain about being able to find somebody who is their financial equal.

They talk about it in terms of the financial relationship. I think if you have a guy who is competitive and has the big ego, more than you can massage and soothe the beast, it's gonna be a problem in the relationship. I can see that in one of my sons because he is so competitive. He wants to be the best at everything. I don't know if I can prep him or change him. That's just who he is, so I don't think that type of relationship would work for him.

I think in trying to not emasculate the husband, sometimes women in these relationships stuff some of their feelings in the closet—right or wrong. There are times that you just have to swallow it and go on. It's a sacrifice that I've chosen to make. I hope I'll choose to make it for ever and ever, but I can see how you might not want to do it forever. It's hard, but I just kind of do it; for example, if I want to buy something expensive and he says, "You can't do that because we don't have money for it." I say, "I go to work every day and I think I should be able to buy what I want." So, I may be pissed off for a couple of days, but in the end, I understand that it would have been an irrational decision. He has to explain to me where the money has gone to other things that were needed in the household.

11) Do you think that more people are satisfied or dissatisfied with this relationship dynamic and why?

I have one other person in this situation. Her husband is very easygoing. He seems to be about us and not about me. I think they handle their finances differently. They seem to be satisfied. She is the one person I can call during some of my breakdown moments because nobody else is going to understand.

12) Is trust, support, or responsibility a factor in your relationship?

Support, when I have to travel—he says, "Well, can't somebody else go?" I say, "No, that's why I'm [in charge]. That's what comes along with the job and the paycheck." Sometimes he forgets to support why I have to do certain things and he's just being selfish and wants me at home. Overall, he is very proud, but sometimes he forgets and I just have to remind him. For us, we had a long time to figure ourselves through the domestic piece. He does the laundry—he's not so efficient and I help sometimes, but sometimes I purposely don't help because it's not my responsibility. I say, "Well, I have enough underwear and my clothes have gone to the cleaners, so I'm good." If they don't have anything, that's on them, because it's his responsibility, so he'll get to it in his time. And I have to be OK with him not doing it in my time.

Now he has the responsibility of [car-pooling the kids]. So, he has the kids and they are saying, "I'm hungry," and he has to take of them. He has never had to do that before—this is a huge responsibility shift for him. I appreciate him doing that. There are times when he has shortcomings and then there are times when he does things like this and I remember why I love him.

13) What advice would you give to other women who may be entering a similar arrangement?

I would probably tell them to figure out if they can handle it. Can they handle being breadwinner, homemaker, wife, caretaker? Realistically, think about what each of those responsibilities is, and if not, they may want to rethink who they are mating with. Just realize that it's hard. And it doesn't get any easier unless he comes up and he's making the same dollar amount, and that their relationship and how they discuss it with their friends is different—but don't feel ashamed about it—don't feel bad about doing well.

14) Is there communication within your marriage or is this topic like the elephant in the room?

I think we communicate well on the topic. I think we have a good relationship on it. Not that we agree on stuff all the time.

15) Does making more money equate to having more of a voice in the relationship?

I don't think so. I don't feel that making more money gives you more of a voice for the man or for the woman. However, I do know that there are men that think they get more say because they make more money. I don't believe that's true. If you have a valid partnership, and that partnership is not 50/50, in my opinion, I don't care who makes more or what, it's not about equal money. It's about feeling equal in a relationship, not even about an equal split of duties. It's how you make each other feel in terms of valuing each other, so I don't think you get more say.

16) What do you need from your mate that you are not getting? What do you think your mates needs from you?

Yes, that's where the conversations came up about picking up more—doing more around the house. In a way, I guess, yeah, my expectations did change. I can't do all that and this.

For me, I can probably say I need consistent support of understanding why I have to work late. Or, why I have to work on days when I would traditionally be off. Or, why I have to work when the kids go to bed. Sometimes I need more understanding.

As for him, I think I give it all—he may think differently about it. I think he gets the support to do his business ventures—and contracting. I play the pretty wife on his arm when we have to go out. I play the role of wife. I'm sure there are times when he wants more of my time and I say, "Look, [.....], I gotta work." So, I guess there are times when he wants more of me and I can't give it because I am spent; I am burned out for the day.

17) What can your mate do to smooth over some of the bumps in the road with regards to salary differences?

I think the overall would be put yourself in her shoes. How would you want her to treat you if you were the main breadwinner? Stop thinking about it in terms of your ego. If you can be her, and she's you, would you want her to do this around the house? Would you want her to support you? Would you want her to brag on you to your friends? Treat her the way you would want her to treat you. Then your relationship will probably be stronger. You can't make her feel guilty about being a success.

Interview #6: Teresa

1) When you entered into this relationship, did you know that you would be earning more? What made you comfortable with that? How did your mate feel about this dynamic? How do you feel about this situation now compared to when you entered the relationship?

I knew it, but what made me comfortable was that we are in our 60s. So, I didn't think it would be as big an issue. I was wrong. He feels bad about it. We were in counseling last summer and the counselor asked, "Does she need you to pay bills or any of those types of things? Does she need you financially? And if you leave, will it impact her financially?" And he said, "No, no, no," and I think it felt like an unnecessary appendage at that point.

I just see that it is such an issue. It came up this morning, he said, "I don't know anything about your portfolio or real estate or the money you have." I didn't say anything because I said it's not going to happen, because it's such an issue, I'm just not going to tell him. My motto is: I don't need anybody to help me do bad—I can do bad all by myself. So, I guess that's where that came from, so I don't talk money.

2) How does this arrangement with you as the breadwinner make you feel?

Well, now it makes me feel nervous, because I have to be patient and let him buy things he can buy, and I'm not the total breadwinner. We were engaged, but I called off the engagement. It was partly financial. It's created two single people living together because he wanted me to put his name on the house that I just bought, and I wasn't going to do that after some things happened. It didn't protect all my 37 years of teaching and education—so I called it off.

Had it been my first relationship, I may have been more willing to share the house. We live and learn, and I knew that it wasn't gonna work like that. It wasn't fair to my children. If I come over and start being friends with, you know I don't expect you to put me in your will, and I don't think it's automatic at this point in my life. Men say that's why they choose younger women, because having the money gives you control over your life that you might not have. If I want something, I can pretty much go out and get it, so if that's what I want and it's my money, I don't have to take into consideration someone else's and their goals.

3) Do you feel comfortable with your family and friends knowing that you earn more? Why or why not?

No, I don't feel comfortable. My family made a really big deal out of it. They instantly assumed that any man [I] was with who didn't have as much as I [had] was with me for the money, and my inheritance, and what the family has put together as a group. I once told a lie that he has property that he doesn't have. I said that to back my family up. It has come back to haunt to big time. Trust me on that.

My advice on dealing with the family—it depends on the age of the person. If you are just starting out and are building something together, that's something they do together. But if you are older with past lives, marriages, children, it is the assumption that each one is bringing something to the table. I think it's kind of tricky because your family is going to be there regardless— through the good, bad, or ugly. They will be there to support you or to rub your nose in it—one or the other, so you have to tread carefully; you also don't want to put the guy in a bad light so he is never thought of as a man. That he's always going to be Mr. so-and-so. I will never change my maiden name again. Ever again. So when people meet you, they assume I'm using his name and they call him Mr. ____, and that really grates on his nerves.

The financial thing is really, really serious. And I think, in my old age, a pre-nupt is really going to have to happen. I finally realize that marriages and relationships are like business and you have to treat them that way. That's ugly

4) What feelings do you hide about this relationship dynamic that you can never tell him?

That it pisses me off that he can never take me on a trip and pay for all of it. I always have to pay part of it. And I think he punishes me because I'm more careful with my money. My attitude about money is different from his. His attitude is you live for today because you don't know if you are going to live tomorrow, and that's true in part, but I believe you need [to] have a little money for cushion. He jabs at me because I'm the one who will buy the generic brands rather than the regular brands, and so he pokes at me about that.

5) What does "head of household" mean to you? Who is the head of the household in your home?

The head of household is the person who makes the final decision. After a discussion is had, if I say I want to go to the beach and he wants to go to the mountains, who makes the final decision and takes the final responsibility for it? I really endeavor to try to defer to him in those types of decisions. I would not call him head of household because, on taxes and money, we file separate taxes. When I can, I try to refer to him as head of household.

6) Would you consider leaving your career behind if it was causing your relationship to suffer?

I'm retired and I've been in this relationship for [several] years. I sort of left the job for caretaking for my dad who was terminally ill. I would not have left a job for this relationship. I educated myself and worked hard [and] enjoyed what I did. I was at the top of my game, so no. I feel that if I have five dollars and you have two, we have seven together. Neither of us would have that separately.

7) What are your overall expectations of a partner/spouse in a relationship? If those expectations have not been met, what do you think has prevented this?

Well, I expected more homogeneity at sixty than at fifty but the problems are the same regardless of the age. It's the attitude [of] what is important [and] what is not important. I thought we would put money into a pot and pay household bills, and then have our separate money. One is that I have more money, and he knows that if he doesn't put the money in, I will take up the slack because he knows it's my house. Two, it's kind of a punishment from him for me not putting his name on my house.

It's completely different from my parents' relationship. It's a cross I bear of shame. My parents were married till death do them part. They were from [the South]. My mother went to college and my father was in the [military], and they built a small empire. My father left us a good bit of money, property, and a lot of cash money—my brother and me—it wasn't a fortune, but considering his education, it was a good amount and I feel that I have to do at least that well with all the resources and opportunities that I have had.

My parents earned about the same. My mother was a stay-at-home housewife till we were in grade school, then went back and got a California teaching credential, and they worked together and built everything, and I feel ashamed that I don't have that type of relationship.

8) What did you get married?

When I was young, I got married for love. When you wanna have children, I believe you need to be married. I am not married now because I feel I would be worse off if I get married. That's harsh, huh?

9) If you have children, what type of individual do you want them to marry? Is it different from your relationship and why?

I want them to be married to people who are equal. I now, in my older age, understand what the Bible means to not become unequally yoked. You should be married to someone who has the same values and goals—that's the key—it doesn't matter about ethnicity as much as it does about a class expectation.

10) Do you think that more people are satisfied or dissatisfied with this relationship dynamic and why?

I think we are resentful and somewhat distressed, and some women are mean about it. My friends feel we have gotten our education and made all the sacrifices to get where we are now. To be fair, some men lost some things in divorce, and so he doesn't have them anymore. Buts it's not our fault, and so later in life you meet men who don't have them anymore—you don't have someone who can bring to the table what you can bring to the table.

Some of my girlfriends are more willing to put everything they have on the table and some of us [are] not. Some of my girlfriends have been in similar relationships and it didn't work out so they are not willing to put everything on the table.

11) Is trust, support, or responsibility a factor in your relationship?

Trust is an issue in my relationship. This is one of my two luggage pieces that I carry. I don't know. I've been down to nothing before with my first husband. I went from teaching to food stamps, because he went out the door and never came back. My second husband had a very prestigious job, [but] lost his job. We made a lot of money when other people didn't have much—then he lost his job due to drinking and we lost a house, boat, motorcycle, all this stuff. We lost everything and I ended up going back home. So I'm not doing that a third time.

I encourage my daughter who has a [young child]—she had the luxury to be a stay-at-home mom—but I encourage her to put away some money on [her] own. I feel a little guilty because I love my son-in-law, but I feel she needs to protect herself. She saw me struggle, work hard, and go the bank and somebody has taken all of your money. That makes you wanna kill somebody.

First marriage, my husband was in the military young, and I was just starting teaching and we were equally yoked. But his attitude was the problem. I was trying to budget and he was trying to spend it all.

Second marriage, my husband made so much more money that he called my money "shoeshine money," but when he lost his job, and then for five years we had to live on my shoeshine money, he sued the company and won, but he developed an alternative lifestyle and I couldn't hold it together anymore.

In this relationship, I feel like I am a contributor to it falling apart because I am not willing to go down certain roads again. He wants me to start fresh and trust him. The thing that's good is we can talk about stuff but it's bad because if we get married, it opens all my assets to community property, everything to a 50/50 split, and I'm just not doing that.

12) What advice would you give to other women who may be entering a similar arrangement?

I would encourage women to seek financial planning before they say "I do" and get a pre-nupt. And I mean that seriously.

If a man is in a situation where he is in medical or law school, and he has the potential to make equal or more, or a blue collar who also has the potential to make more—I still think nowadays women and men need to be smart and go to financial counseling and pre-nuptial arrangements, and go to counseling for child rearing. I think those things can really mess up a relationship.

My advice is: Can you get a reference from a past girlfriend? Can you pass a credit check? Can you bring a clean AIDS test? Watch how much he drinks. How does he treat wait staff? How does he treat other people? I could not have a boyfriend who doesn't support his children. I would watch how he talks about his mom and past women.

13) Is there communication within your marriage or is this topic like the elephant in the room?

It's sometimes the elephant in the room. He will jab about it, so it's more of an issue for him than it is to me. But I receive the jab, so then it's an issue for me. He will make the statement in company, "Women are selfish with their money, they don't want share what they have," referring to me not wanting to put his name on stuff that he hasn't earned: my house.

One time we went on a trip and he said, "You never pay your way." We had a big argument about that and he said he was just angry, that's why he said that, and I said, "I've bailed you out more than once. Who rented the car? Who did this; who did that?" If I didn't go on the trip, then he wouldn't be able to go in the style he likes to go on trips. I'm moderate. If we get a room that doesn't have roaches, is clean, then I'm good to good—he has to have luxury, a suite or whatever—well, if you like to do that, then you have to pay to be the boss. One time we went on a trip and he sat in first class and I was in coach. I think he should have upgraded my ticket—he told me I was just being cheap. That I could have paid for first class.

14) Does making more money equate to having more of a voice in the relationship?

Not necessarily. With two adults, you know the person with the most money can make the decisions. [But] we have to somewhat save our men's self-esteem. I have more money, but let us make this decision together. I think that women should [have] their own money that doesn't go into the pot.

15) How has your current dynamic affected your expectations for your spouse and his "role" in the marriage?

I have mixed feelings. Yes and no. I would expect that he would take me out for meals, but I would do the same for him. My mother says the only time a lady goes in her purse is to get lipstick not [her] credit card. Now, sometimes, I just sit there because I'm just not going to do it.

He doesn't make a lot of payments on the house and stuff. He does a lot of stuff in the house, but he doesn't pay, so I feel he has enough money to take me out and treat me. But he seems to want to extract that money out of me a little. I'm the kind of person who doesn't like a lot of bickering over money at the table, so I'll just pay for the meal.

Before we go out, I'll say, "Look, do you have enough money? Do we need to stop at the bank?" Or, if it's impromptu, then I'll get up to go the bathroom and give the waiter my card to charge the meal, and then I just pay for the meal.

16) What do you need from your mate that you are not getting? What do you think your mates needs from you?

I need support and appreciation. I want to be appreciated. I don't need all that other stuff. I want to be supported in my endeavors. I just started two small network businesses. I like to be accepted for who I am. That's what I need from him. I need support when I don't need finances—I can buy what I want.

All women need to do is give men sex and a little pat on the head and everything is OK. I think he wants a lot more sex and he would get it if he didn't piss me off all the time. He wants unflagging adoration. He always went out with young women and they looked up to him and thought he was so great, but you can't tell a woman sixty-some years old just any crazy thing.

17) What can your mate do to smooth over some of the bumps in the road with regards to salary differences?

They have to become financially educated so they can make investments, do savings, make out a financial plan for the family or the couple, and stay with it, and help the family stick to the plan, and gain financial independence. I would be highly respectful and grateful. A man who says these are our goals and sees that the family sticks to it—learn about investments, that he leads the way.

You need to look at the big picture –resists the buying fancy cars and living in an apartment—that's stupid—teach their children it's not about what you're wearing or what you're sporting but how to be smart about how you look at money.

In this relationship, we could live on one salary and bank the other. We could be balling but he's going to say it's because I won't open up my finances. It's not totally true. I put my money in our joint account. I don't have access to his personal account at all. He's a gentleman. Give credit where it's due.

Interview #7: Annette

1) When you entered into this relationship, did you know that you would be earning more? What made you comfortable with that? How did your mate feel about this dynamic? How do you feel about this situation now compared to when you entered the relationship?

No, I didn't know I was going to be earning more. My husband was laid off a couple of years ago from a [blue collar] field.

Honestly, nothing is said—he feels like I run the household because I make the most money.

2) How does this arrangement with you as the breadwinner make you feel?

I feel different. When you get married, you think that your husband would be the breadwinner and when that doesn't happen, it makes you feel uncomfortable.

He's not as outspoken as he was before when he was the main breadwinner. We [separated] because of it. I feel like his personality changed.

3) Do you feel comfortable with your family and friends knowing that you earn more? Why or why not?

It's nothing that I discuss with family and friends. My closest friends know that I make more money. It's nothing that I discuss because I am a personal type person. I have a very small circle of friends. I mostly keep it to myself. I am not ashamed to discuss it, it's just my personality.

4) What feelings do you hide about this relationship dynamic that you can never tell him?

OK. Well, I guess how I really feel—I feel I'm the only person putting toward the family. I don't feel like [he's] cutting it for me. He's not contributing to the household as much as he could.

5) What does "head of household" mean to you? Who is the head of the household in your home?

I think it was shared when we were together. Now that we are not together. To me, head of household is the person trying to hold down the house. Having to work and then coming home to take care of the kids and the house.

When he was laid off, I became the decision-maker as to what was going on. I'm a go-getter, so whatever I have to do, I'm going to do to keep the household running. He's laid back. There are issues that are going on that are not really bothering him. Because I'm there now, it's solely my problem. I think he just gave up. He's a very prideful person and so because he was not in control, he just stepped away from the situation.

6) Would you consider leaving your career behind if it was causing your relationship to suffer?

I would not give up my career. We dated before I was in [this field] but, in the beginning of my marriage, I think he was intimidated or not so happy with me, by me choosing [this] as a profession even though that's what I went to school for. I would not leave my job—I have too much invested. I only have two more years before I can retire.

7) What are your overall expectations of a partner/spouse in a relationship? If those expectations have not been met, what do you think has prevented this?

My expectations are to have someone [I] can sit down and talk [with] about how our household needs to run, and about the kids as far as their education, and so forth.

My expectations were not met because he was too wrapped up in himself and his family. When he first left his job, I talked to him about leaving [...] to go someplace else to seek a job. So, we wouldn't be in the situation that we are in now. But he refused because he had older grandparents who reared him.

He felt obligated to take care of them, but when they passed, it was nothing really holding him here. His grandfather had a spouse at that time, and when he passed, then he felt obligated to take care of her; she had her own children, he was just a grandchild. So, I think it was selfishness on his part of not taking his own family and household into consideration in that decision that he made.

I wanted him to [relocate temporarily] until things picked back up in [his] industry. So, he got laid off and he's working for money that he got when he was in college, basically. And my suggestion was you can get on with the company you've been with, out in the West somewhere, and me and the kids could just commute [back and forth], but he was more worried about what was going to happen with his grandparents.

8) How similar is your relationship to your parents' relationship? Is that acceptable to you?

- My mother wasn't married when I came about; she was divorced. I didn't have the know-how about how a relationship was supposed to work because I didn't see one with my mom. She kept her private life very private. I didn't know how it was supposed to work. I just jumped into it and worked it the way I thought it was supposed to work.

I don't think he really likes that characteristic about me—he doesn't like that I'm as assertive as I am, but that's the kind of mother that I had, and I saw what she had to do to make sure that we had [what we needed]. So I got that characteristic from her.

9) Why did you get married or enter into a long-term relationship?

I got married because [I] loved him as a person and I thought we would do well as a family, rearing kids and things of that nature.

10) If you have children, what type of individual do you want them to marry? Is it different from your relationship and why?

I would not discourage it. I don't think a relationship or marriage is based on who makes the most money. I think it's based on how you feel about that person and how that person feels about you. I think it's important that you have a common goal and work together towards that goal. That's all that's important.

11) Do you think that more people are satisfied or dissatisfied with this relationship dynamic and why?

Well, I think most of the young ladies in my circle are not married, most are divorced, but I don't think they have a problem with that type of relationship.

12) Is trust, support, or responsibility a factor in your relationship?

I would say responsibility was an issue. Me being the mother, I always felt that I was the one who was more responsible for the kids. I would have to tell him what I wanted. And like a mother, you just see what needs to be done and you do it. So, I think it was responsibility.

13) Would you encourage others to have the same relationship dynamic? Why or why not?

A relationship is not based off of who makes the most money. If that person loves the other person and the other person loves them and respects them, I would encourage them to move forward even with the roles being reversed.

14) What advice would you give to other women who may be entering a similar arrangement?

My advice would be to let them know that there will be unsaid things. He may not ever open his mouth to say that he feels maybe less of a man because he makes less, but just to let her know that those things will come up whether he says it with his mouth or with his actions. And once she sees it, go ahead and discuss it with him.

15) Is there communication within your marriage or is this topic like the elephant in the room?

We didn't discuss it. It was more of [a] "Let's just work through it" deal. Maybe if we had discussed it, I wouldn't be in the position I'm in now.

16) Does making more money equate to having more of a voice in the relationship?

I think it should be a joint venture. One person should not have more say-so than the other person, especially when both people are working. Both people have feelings and both people should have a voice. Just because he's a man, he supposed to be the head, but women should also have a voice. If you are a housewife, you should not have less voice than a woman who is going out to work every day.

17) How has your current dynamic affected your expectations for your spouse and his "role" in the marriage?

Yes, I had my kids in private school up until two years ago, after he lost his job. All of the education for my kids was taken care of by me—no one really knew it was taken care of by me—everybody thought it was a joint venture, but it wasn't. I would just go out and work extra jobs to keep them in private school. Things were done where it looked like he was doing it, when, in fact, he wasn't.

18) What do you need from your mate that you are not getting? What do you think your mates needs from you?

When he lost his job, I took on the responsibility of taking care of the household; he just gave up. I worked 12-hour shifts and we have three kids between 11 and 8. He would be responsible for picking them up from school and getting them to the bus. The same things I would be doing if I was off.

I expected him to pick up my role when he wasn't working. Starting them with their homework—he would get them to the bus but he would not do domestic things such as laundry. But he stepped up more when it came to the kids. That was something I didn't have to worry about at that time.

I don't feel as though I was appreciated the way I felt I should have been appreciated. I said, "You can make your mouth say anything, but your actions don't say that you appreciate what I'm trying to do—trying to accomplish." I felt under appreciated.

From me, I think he probably wasn't getting a full understanding of what he was going through. Me understanding the fact that he was used to making a certain amount of dollars and now I'm making this. And during that time, he had two or three deaths in his family. It was a conglomerate of everything attacking us all at once, and me still trying to take care of the house and the kids, and work and try to be emotionally there for him. I don't think—maybe I [wasn't] as sensitive as he needed at that time. I had become desensitized.

19) What can your mate do to smooth over some of the bumps in the road with regards to salary differences?

Well, in reference to finances, if he would work as hard as I would, I don't think he worked as hard as he could have. I would work a 12-hour shift then go work another four hours—a 16-hour day. Then come home and take care of the kids and the house. I felt if he could have put in as much work as I did then we could have survived.

Interview #8: Donna

1) When you entered into this relationship, did you know that you would be earning more? What made you comfortable with that? How did your mate feel about this dynamic? How do you feel about this situation now compared to when you entered the relationship?

No, my husband had a good opportunity working for a company named [...] but they closed up. In my marriage, my husband worked while I went to college. So, his money got us started. Then going through college, and when I got my degree, I went into the business world. I came on board making $5000 more than the person sitting next to me.

My husband ran the finances; I had the baby.

2) How does this arrangement with you as the breadwinner make you feel?

Five years into the marriage, things changed. I never really thought about it. He handled all the finances. I wanted to be a stay-at-home mom. That's the attitude I had through all of it. We bought a home—I had the baby and I did part-time work. Having the responsibility of the house that we both signed on for, I lost the ability to be a stay-at-home mom.

So, throughout the whole thing, I never took the responsibility for the fact that it was happening that way. I never brought it up. I never rubbed it in. I just kept it quiet, which I realize now was a mistake. I should have said something. I did not know I had him by that much money until [it was] time for my daughter to go to college. I realized the salary disparity at that time. I was making over $60,000 and he was making just over $30,000. I had not looked at the finances or the taxes—I just signed my name at tax time. He was dealing with the issue long before I was.

When the baby was seven months old, I got my first paycheck more than his. He [said], "Take the baby and run; you don't need me."

I asked for marriage counseling. In the marriage counseling, he said, "You are a hell of a mother but you are not much of a wife." He said, "You have always been with her,"—meaning my daughter. He told the marriage counselor he saw me as a threat. When it was time for him to do the income taxes, he would throw things and turn things over in the house—chairs and sofas. I remember one time he picked up one of my earrings off the floor and [threw] it down the hall and said, "I am tired of picking up after you." It was at income tax time. He had a really hard time with the income disparity but he was keeping it inside, and I didn't understand it because he didn't talk about it. I saw horrible abuse around us—not to me or to my daughter, but around us.

3) Do you feel comfortable with your family and friends knowing that you earn more? Why or why not?

No, not really. My family and friends were all mothers and their husbands all made more money. He is one of seven children and I am one of four. We are the only relationship that had his happen. All of the couples are still together and still making it because the husband feels like something. Because the man feels like he is needed for that family. I didn't have that.

Even though he was emotionally needed and wanted, he just never felt that he was needed because of the difference in the salaries. The other women I knew didn't have that situation. I was the only one going through that.

4) What feelings do you hide about this relationship dynamic that you can never tell him?

Twice I turned down a salary increase. I worked for a company that didn't pay very much, and they got bought out and we were brought back in, and the company said, "Your salaries are really low," and they gave us a raise and everybody was happy—except me. I took that raise home and I got horrible glares and stares. I received no praise—nothing!! I would go back into the office and say, "Thank you very much, but it's not a good time for me to get a raise." I tried to keep things low-key. My family meant everything to me.

I never saw this dynamic with my parents. My mother was a nurse and my father worked at [.....]. My mother gave up her job to raise the family. My father became the breadwinner for the family. My mother went back to work part time, but my father was always the main breadwinner. My grandfather was the breadwinner and my grandmother was the homemaker. I never saw this type of relationship in my family—the woman being the breadwinner. In my aunts and uncles marriages, I never saw it the way it was happening inside of my marriage.

I was raised with the Dick and Jane books, with here comes Daddy from work and Mommy making the food—the Beaver Cleaver days. That's how I was raised.

5) What does "head of household" mean to you? Who is the head of the household in your home?

My husband controlled the finances. Head of household means to me: who decides where you live; what are you doing with your cars? He was the one who decided how the money was going to be used. The cars that he bought were always very nice cars. In the dealership they would say to me, when he left to go to the bathroom, "It's so sad about his finances." I had to always co-sign for the cars. I always had to agree to everything because of the amount of money I made.

But I never said anything to him about that. Head of household is making those types of decisions. But, my husband made a decision that I went against because he had lost his job and wanted to move us to Ohio because he said he could get a job there. I didn't want to move and take my daughter out of her school. I also loved my job and I didn't want to move. I told him I would come to Ohio but that he should go first. If it had not been for my job, we probably would have gone. He decided not to go. Note: I could never get him to do any household chores. He felt it was demeaning.

6) Would you consider leaving your career behind if it was causing your relationship to suffer?

I did when I lost my job. I got laid off. My husband had moved out because of our separation. I saw a lawyer and the lawyer said, "Be hush-hush, as quiet as you can. Do everything he says, because you are going to have to pay the alimony." I knew my husband was having a problem with the money thing.

So, I sabotaged and I didn't try really hard to get back into my field of work. I didn't want to pay the alimony. I wanted to make my husband feel better about himself even though we were separated. I think a woman should do everything she can for her partner. I went from $37 an hour to a minimum-wage job hoping it would save the marriage.

It made me feel better because I was making less than him, but the marriage was so far gone at that time—it really didn't help out at all. When I look back at it, I'm sorry I did that because now I'm trying to still get back into my profession and it's harder now for me to get back on top. I'm restarting at a much lower salary.

I've had to use my 401k funds now to survive because I took the minimum-wage job, and so now I've got all those penalties, and now I have all types of income tax problems. So, yes, I made the money, I lost the money. I lost the job. The husband ran; I lost the husband. So, I'm just stuck financially.

7) What are your overall expectations of a partner/spouse in a relationship? If those expectations have not been met, what do you think has prevented this?

I expected my husband to be the head of the household. I respected him as a man. I had that feeling inside of myself. I still believe that, but he didn't feel that or believe that. Maybe I should have put my hand on his shoulder when he came home from work and asked, "How did your day go?"

If he was recording our direct deposits into our account and I would see that he made some additional money—overtime or whatever—I would praise him and he would glare at me and roll his eyes because my money being deposited was more than his was. So, I couldn't even praise him. I didn't like the abuse that was going on, the throwing things around the house, turning furniture over. I was never touched, but I didn't have any divorces around me so I didn't want a divorce. I just put up with his behavior.

I didn't like what happened after the baby was born; he wanted a one-on-one with me and not have the child in the picture. But I didn't know how to get out of my situation. I just kept on going.

8) How similar is your relationship to your parents' relationship? Is that acceptable to you?

My mom was not the breadwinner, but she controlled the finances. In my marriage, my husband took charge of the finances. I was very sheltered growing up. My mom never shared a checking account, phone bill—nothing. I saw my father being the decision maker for the family, but my mom was the more domineering one. In my own relationship, it was my husband who was the decision maker.

I don't know why I wasn't more like my mom. I saw the abuse [with my mom and dad]. I saw the fist-fighting and struggling with the abuse. So, when I had it happening, even though I was never touched, I had seen the abuse when I was growing up, so I thought it was OK.

My parents put all of their money together in one big pot. There were not any separate accounts, so in my marriage I thought we should have one big pot, too.

Even now, as we are going through the mediation because of our divorce, I have to continue to let him make all the financial decisions. I have to let him decide about the IRA accounts, etc., and keep my hands out of all of the finances that he put together, because he said if I don't, he will not walk my daughter down the aisle when she gets married. My daughter is 25 years old. To this day there is a deep, deep jealously.

9) *Why did you get married or enter into a long-term relationship?*

My girlfriend was married. Very close girlfriend introduced us. She and her boyfriend were married. I was 22 years old. I felt old at home. College was finished. I had a job. I don't have any stories of a man kneeling down and asking me for marriage. I asked him.

10) *If you have children, what type of individual do you want them to marry? Is it different from your relationship and why?*

My daughter has a college degree and is doing very well. I want her to have the fun and games in her life. She's in a relationship now. He is someone who is financially equivalent to her. I have forewarned her about showing too much attention to any baby she has.

I tell her a lot that I will be taking the baby to babysit so she can have more time with her husband. I will constantly encourage her to have a lot of time with her and her husband and away from the children. Although I think making a happy family unit is the way to go.

11) Do you think that more people are satisfied or dissatisfied with this relationship dynamic and why?

I never saw this type of relationship dynamic with anyone else. Everyone else I knew had the traditional marriage.

12) Is trust, support, or responsibility a factor in your relationship?

He was very responsible and he worked hard; but in all honesty, he was a good guy. My mother thought that he was a hard worker. I never felt that he was untrustworthy.

I was lacking in support from him. I changed jobs. I got a job where I brought my computer home so I could work from home. My husband spent so much time on that computer playing online games, without any regard for the work I had to do for my job on that computer.

My job affected the lives of patients. I worked for a hospital. I often had to call the hospital to see if the patient was dead or alive. He would not get off the computer so I could work. I had to wait for him to go to the bathroom. If the patient was alive, I had to get on the computer. I had to beg and beg to get him off the computer. If the patient was deceased then he could continue to play on the computer. I had to force him off the computer. He had no regard for my job. If I got a call when I was making dinner and had to get on the computer, he would give me such nasty glares and stares.

13) Would you encourage others to have the same relationship dynamic? Why or why not?

I would say, yes—to move forward. The money allows the family the ability to have fun in life and to have nice things; things that don't happen if there is no money. But the money situation has to be talked about. The money I made brought a lot of the nicer things in life—the ability to travel and to have nice cars. I would want all those good things for my daughter. Maybe their relationship would be more of a partnership. Where I was brought up, the husband was the head of family and the wife was subservient. But I believe in the family unit, and I believe a family unit that can only happen when one person is in charge.

I would say I'm torn with my answer because it can destroy a man's self-worth when the wife makes more. I was told by my aunt that marriages from different sides of the track don't work. Look what happened to me—it didn't work. So, what would I say to my daughter? I saw her with a guy who lived up the street who was from the other side of the tracks and she seemed to be having a lot of fun with him. The guy she is engaged to now, I don't see them having as much fun. I am very much torn with the answer for that, because it can destroy a man! It can destroy a man and that's exactly what happened with me. My husband couldn't find the goodness in me. He sat in a chair one time and cried and cried like a baby and said, "I wish I had your job!!"

14) What advice would you give to other women who may be entering a similar arrangement?

I would always say the money issue needs to be talked about. We never know what is going to happen. Here I'm going through a divorce and I don't have any savings account. I made $37,000 more than my husband for several years. What happened to that money? Where is my savings account? I don't have it. I would say don't ever let yourself get into a situation like me. The family's finances have to be on a spreadsheet—written in black and white. The spreadsheet has to show what money is coming into the household and how it's being spent.

Women have to save for a rainy day! You never know when the husband may leave. Prepare yourself! Inform yourself about the family finances. Be a partner—don't be subservient!

Make time for just you and your husband away from your child. It's important to get away alone as a couple.

15) Is there communication within your marriage or is this topic like the elephant in the room?

We did not talk about the money difference in our home—Even though he handled the finances. I really wanted to be a stay-at-home Mom, but it never happened.

16) What do you need from your mate that you are not getting? What do you think your mates needs from you?

I felt my husband should have tried harder to make more of himself. I wanted him to be what he wanted to be. I don't think he could ever find what he wanted to be. I could never get him to do anything around the house—the cooking, cleaning, etc.—I didn't want to make him feel like any less of a man.

17) What can your mate do to smooth over some of the bumps in the road with regards to salary differences?

Become more involved in the marriage. Be willing to go into her office and shut the door and have some private time. Get on board and travel with her and support her in her job. If she is traveling, go with her and try to enjoy her job. Make some time together as she travels. Talk about the income differences. Find something the two of you can do together.

Allow the wife to share information about her job with you. Try to pull your wife away from the work sometimes so she does not get too absorbed in it. Make the home be her place away from her job.

Interview #9: Francine

1) When you entered into this relationship, did you know that you would be earning more? What made you comfortable with that? How did your mate feel about this dynamic? How do you feel about this situation now compared to when you entered the relationship?

Yes, I think because the disparity of the income was not that much. He was the same because we were so close. We had the conversation early on about what grade are you? It wasn't something that we dwelled on. We have our challenges but it's not based on the income because our difference in salaries is not that great. I think if the income had been greater it would have been more of an issue for both of us.

2) How does this arrangement with you as the breadwinner make you feel?

I don't really know if I agree that I'm the breadwinner. I feel I don't have the flexibility to say I wanna quit and come home and be a full-time mom. But I guess that's the biggest issue. We can't make it off of his salary, as far as our standard of living.

3) Do you feel comfortable with your family and friends knowing that you earn more? Why or why not?

Most people don't know—I believe my parents know, but not the exact figures. The majority of my friends don't know. I think it's none of their business. We just don't talk about salaries.

4) What feelings do you hide about this relationship dynamic that you can never tell him?

I'm not hiding any feeling about it. We've had discussions [about] it. In his case, his career field is not as much in demand, so he is stuck [commuting] to maintain his salary. Our child is the reason I don't want to commute. I feel like I'm being left behind in this field because my colleagues are now making more money than me because they are working in [another] area. But that doesn't have anything to do with him.

5) What does "head of household" mean to you? Who is the head of the household in your home?

Head of household is a leader but not a dictator. In our relationship, [he] is the head of household. Initially when we got married, we lived in my house that I had previously purchased. Now we live in the house in his name and he is fully invested in the household. He has accepted more responsibility now than he did in our previous house. I am from a traditional standpoint. I grew up thinking that the man is the head of the household, so that's kind of how I feel.

I feel a woman who does not bring any money into the household [gives] up some of her rights. If she is dependent on him to get her nails done, then how can she have the say so? My grandmothers did not work, and my grandfathers paid the bills, and the grandmothers were disempowered. My grandmother could not even drive. Now it's totally flipped and I'm making so much more money than my grandmothers and a little more than my husband, so it's different than it was 50 years ago.

6) Would you consider leaving your career behind if it was causing your relationship to suffer?

No, but if he could afford to maintain our household and have the same standard of living. I would love to be a housewife. If he said, "You can't work at all," then no because that would be giving up a lot of power.

7) What are your overall expectations of a partner/spouse in a relationship? If those expectations have not been met, what do you think has prevented this?

I expect my spouse to be a supporter of me, my cheerleader, be there for my emotional support. They are a partner in our life together. They are someone I can depend on. They are a protector of me and my family. I think they have been met. It's never 100-percent all the time, but it ebbs and flows. Overall, expectations are met.

8) How similar is your relationship to your parents' relationship? Is that acceptable to you?

It's not similar at all. My parent's marriage is very dysfunctional. My father has always been the breadwinner and so it's totally flipped—the mortgage is in his name only. He pays the mortgage himself. Whereas, we went into our mortgage 50/50. In the past, I may have used their relationship as a model as far as selection of men goes. But now I've done some soul searching and I can see what's going on as an adult and it's a good thing we are not like that. The difference is acceptable. I don't want to use their relationship as a model. I think it's good that my marriage is not like that.

9) Why did you get married or enter into a long-term relationship?

When we got married, I was pregnant. We had been together for [several] years. I felt we were already acting like a married couple so why not get married. I didn't want to continue in the relationship without the benefits of marriage. I felt it was more beneficial financially; we could [share] expenses and do more as a married couple than as two single people. And yes, we did love each other.

10) If you have children, what type of individual do you want them to marry? Is it different from your relationship and why?

I want her to marry someone who treats her like a queen and encourages her to be her best. I would love it if she could find someone who was rich, but I don't want her to be disempowered. I don't want her to be overly dependent on a man. I'd rather have her be with someone who is on the same level as her. So, if she's [affluent], she can get with [someone who is affluent]. If she's not, I would be a little concerned about how his family looks at her. I think it's easier if you are [on] the same level as far as how you were raised.

11) Do you think that more people are satisfied or dissatisfied with this relationship dynamic and why?

I don't see it as being a huge issue among my friends. I don't see it in my family's relationships.

12) Is trust, support, or responsibility a factor in your relationship?

It has been but it's more of an ebb and flow. Things surfaced that called into question that area, but it's not a constant thing. It's not a main issue with us.

13) Would you encourage others to have the same relationship dynamic? Why or why not?

I would advise that the disparity be no more than $10,000. If the woman does earn more, it should not be that much more.

14) What advice would you give to other women who may be entering a similar arrangement?

I think if you encourage your man to be head of household, you have to include him in household decisions and not just run off and do something because you make more money.

15) Is there communication within your marriage or is this topic like the elephant in the room?

It's a non-issue. We just don't talk about it because the disparity is so little.

16) How has your current dynamic affected your expectations for your spouse and his "role" in the marriage? Does the fact that you make more change your expectations of his duties around the house?

[He] does his share so we don't have that issue. He is former [military], so he's really good about keeping the house in order. He is not a neat freak, but when it's time to clean, he does a very good job.

17) Do you ever feel the need to overcompensate for the difference in your income?

No, I will publicly give him the bank card or cash in front of everybody. There is no hiding. And he's OK with that.

18) What do you need from your mate that you are not getting? What do you think your mates needs from you?

Just the fact that I don't have a choice to not work. I don't feel any aspect of our relationship that is not being met due to the disparity in income. I don't give off a sense of neediness. So, maybe I might come off as being bossy or about business and not as soft if he would like me to be.

19) What can your mate do to smooth over some of the bumps in the road with regards to salary differences?

I don't really think there is anything that he can do. We [have a small] salary difference, so there is not anything I can think of.

Interview #10: Emma

1) When you entered into this relationship, did you know that you would be earning more? What made you comfortable with that? How did your mate feel about this dynamic?

How do you feel about this situation now compared to when you entered the relationship?

Yes, I did know I would be earning more, but I knew my husband had the potential to grow in his job. I had no idea that my income would take off the way that it did. I was able to triple his income.

It was not an issue at first—I think he thought that his earning potential was great and he would be able to surpass my income. We didn't have an open discussion about it.

Now we are at a point where we are getting separated. It's actually the best thing for both of us—we don't have any children, we don't have any joint assets together—no one plans on it ending up this way but it is what it is, and I think at the end of the day we are both comfortable with our decision. I initiated it, of course. I think money and finances and communication had something to do with it.

I really never had a problem with the disparity in income as long as my husband was able to provide me the things that I needed in the marriage to make it work. Let's be honest—all women want a husband who is secure financially and other ways. I would love to have had that opportunity—it's never too late.

But, I don't look at the money as the main factor in determining my mate. As long as that person can balance a budget and make wise choices and is able to maintain their part of the budget, I really don't care.

2) How does this arrangement with you as the breadwinner make you feel?

I'm always in a position where I feel like I'm the head. I would love to have some help, because I am the major breadwinner. I feel like it's always my responsibility to see that all of the bills are paid, and paid on time. Because my background is financial, he just expected me to take that role because it's more comfortable for me than it is for him. He doesn't really pay bills on time and he knows how I am about paying bills on time.

3) Do you feel comfortable with your family and friends knowing that you earn more? Why or why not?

I don't tell anybody I make more. They can just tell from the outside looking in when my husband's friends will come over, especially the women. However, they automatically assume that he is the breadwinner and I am just reaping the benefits. Women often assume that just because you live in a certain place or have certain things, that the man is the breadwinner. I think that is distressing.

My friends know that I am the breadwinner because my husband will sometimes say that I picked out everything—my friends know [me]. They know that I'm a nurturer; that I like to make the house a home; they know my standards; they know if I see something I like I'm going to get it. I can't explain how they know, but they just know. Or they may hear me say certain things about how my husband wasn't responsible. His family is in another state. I don't know if they have any perception—his mom may know—he doesn't have a big family.

4) What feelings do you hide about this relationship dynamic that you can never tell him?

I won't tell my husband my salary. If he really knew how much I made—I don't think he could handle it. Or I just feel that he could not handle it mentally. If he makes a comment about him not knowing how much money I make, I say, "I don't think you really need to know that as long as the bills get paid."

Also when people feel like you make a certain amount of money, it gives them more leeway to be less responsible—I didn't want him to be less responsible financially. I want him to say, "Even though she makes that amount of money, I still need to bring my share to the table." We were in a place where my husband would short me in terms of what he would give me for the household items and I felt that if he knew how much I made he would be worse. That's really why I didn't tell him.

I don't really hold in my feelings from my husband. I just need to get my feelings out. In a relationship, you just need to be honest about how you feel. He knows how I feel about everything. Even though I was communicating my feelings, I didn't get any results.

After a few years [without results], I wanted a dialogue and he thought that I was complaining. I would say, "No, I'm not complaining. This is important." That's why I'm ending the marriage and going on with my life.

5) What does "head of household" mean to you? Who is the head of the household in your home?

The head of the household is the person who leads the household. I consider myself the head of the household. My husband is one of those people who just goes with the flow. I think sometimes he doesn't want to challenge me. I'm very open minded which is why I don't understand why we don't have dialogue. He'll just say, "yes, yes," anything just to get me to be quiet.

6) Would you consider leaving your career behind if it was causing your relationship to suffer?

I have never considered leaving my career behind, but I have considered working less if it would make the marriage work. That's something that I definitely would have done if he wanted that. I have never had a discussion about trying to make it off of one income, we probably could have done it, but it's just not something that we ever considered.

7) What are your overall expectations of a partner/spouse in a relationship? If those expectations have not been met, what do you think has prevented this?

I think a spouse should be open and honest about everything even if it's something bad because I think if you harbor those feelings it just make things worse—I always wanted my spouse to be my friend. I wanted us to be the same way we were when we were courting. I think living together with life's challenges you forget the basic things we should be doing in a relationship.

I want my spouse to do the manly things in the house—the outside chores—that's important to me. I don't care if he hires somebody, but he needs to see that the outside chores are done. I don't mind doing the cooking, cleaning, laundry, etc.—the womanly things. I don't mind doing that, but I want my spouse to be financially responsible. I just want basic stuff. I like surprises. I don't need expensive stuff. I would like to come home and have dinner cooked every once in a while. Or just to go out for dinner—just those small quiet moments are important to me.

8) How similar is your relationship to your parents' relationship? Is that acceptable to you?

My parents didn't have a great marriage, so I probably wouldn't use their marriage as a barometer. I saw financial stability in my mother. My father was financially irresponsible and so actually my marriage is just like my mom's in that respect—and the communication and the honesty. So, that's a little deep—I didn't even realize that before.

9) Why did you get married or enter into a long-term relationship?

I got married because I loved my husband. I thought we would make a great team. And he embodied those attributes that I thought would be good for a husband. Along the way things got lost because—he got involved in activities and I started [my career]. We just got busy with life—it's a two-way street. I don't want to make it seem like it was one sided.

10) If you have children, what type of individual do you want them to marry? Is it different from your relationship and why?

I would tell my daughter to go with her heart in choosing a mate, and she'll figure it out. I would not tell her either way.

11) Do you think that more people are satisfied or dissatisfied with this relationship dynamic and why?

I think men love women as breadwinners because it gives them a crutch. Some of them do; some of them are takers. I think women don't like it. We want to be taken care of. That's my perception.

12) Is trust, support, or responsibility a factor in your relationship?

All three are issues in my relationship. If he were the breadwinner, I think the issues would be the same.

13) Would you encourage others to have the same relationship dynamic? Why or why not?

I would encourage women to have dialogue about it prior to marriage. They can go from there. Most people don't have the dialogue.

14) What advice would you give to other women who may be entering a similar arrangement?

I would advise women to get counseling before getting into this type of marriage. That's important. Discuss all the dynamics beforehand and how they would handle it. It's hard for the man and for the woman. We had counseling at the church but it wasn't the right type. I think all couples need financial counseling and marital counseling before marriage, whether they are in good financial shape or not.

15) Is there communication within your marriage or is this topic like the elephant in the room?

It was the elephant in the room. I don't think either one of us thought it was a problem. In terms of what we both put on the table monthly toward the bills—to this day—it's still 50/50. So, it's not like I was paying more. As long as that [was] happening, I was ok with that. My husband lost his job and I had to support us for two years.

What made me decide to get a separation is because when he got his job, I had to carry everything for two years which was significant for me—in a recession—and having done that, it put me in a bad position with the IRS. I had to pay the IRS, because I was trying to keep a roof over our heads.

When my husband got a job, I asked him for a couple hundred extra dollars a month so I could pay a monthly payment to the IRS. His answer was so just not what I expected. So, I said, "OK, we are supposed to be in a marriage where we work together, and I made it all happen when you didn't have a job, and you can't help me now."

He said when he was unemployed I wouldn't give him $20. I said, "Well, I had to pay extra [money every] month, and when you are an able-bodied man and turned down temp jobs and other jobs that you could have had because you were too proud, and you wanted me to give you money like I'm your mother—I'm your wife, not your mother—I felt like I was doing my part."

He could have done other things around the house—making sure the house is clean, cooking, the laundry; he sat around feeling sorry for himself. He told me I didn't know how it feels to be fired, but I said, "You still have to provide for your family." I gave him some time, but after a while, I said, "You have to dust yourself off and get up."

When he said he wouldn't help me, I said, "Well, OK, I know what I have to do."

16) Does making more money equate to having more of a voice in the relationship?

No, I don't think it should give the woman more of a voice. I think everybody's situation is going to be different. I feel that we should have a household where we contribute equally.

17) Do you ever feel the need to overcompensate for the difference in your income?

There are some times when I overcompensated. We were on vacation, and we saw some things we wanted so I just went ahead and bought [them] for him. I didn't give him the money because he is financially irresponsible; we had a joint credit card at one time, but he didn't know how to handle it so I closed the account.

If we were going out with another couple, I would ask ahead of time if he had the money because I don't like surprises. If he has it, he will take care of it. His preference is to pay if he's in front of other people.

18) What do you need from your mate that you are not getting? What do you think your mates needs from you?

I would love for my husband to say, "Let's go on vacation," and pay for it. We both always have to pay. I would have to say responsibilities for the man regardless of the income.

I think I needed more of his time. We didn't have enough time together. Respect. I needed more communication. I would communicate my feelings and he didn't respond; it makes the woman feel like her concerns are not valid. She feels like she is being brushed off to the side. Men need to listen more.

I think my husband needs more of my time. He would probably say affection.

19) What can your mate do to smooth over some of the bumps in the road with regards to salary differences?

That's easy. Spend more time. Talking. Honesty. I need somebody to be honest. I hate being lied to. Communicate. As women, we don't always know what the man is thinking. We just make assumptions on what we think they are thinking. Men need to be more responsible and step up to the plate. I don't know if it's being lazy. I think sometimes men have just gotten by with so much in life and women just accepting those faults, so they don't feel they have to work on them.

Interview # 11: Gina

1) When you entered into this relationship, did you know that you would be earning more? What made you comfortable with that? How did your mate feel about this dynamic? How do you feel about this situation now compared to when you entered the relationship?

Actually, no, we got married after we had just finished college. He made more than I did. We are in different careers paths and so it changed over time that I made more. We never had a discussion about salaries.

The situation was never discussed. He felt good about being the major breadwinner in the household. We never discussed salary potential.

2) How does this arrangement with you as the breadwinner make you feel?

Initially I used to downplay it and not discuss it and change my spending habits to the point of not having my spending reflect my salary, but over the years I felt if I'm making this money then I need to definitely enjoy it and live the lifestyle I can afford.

In the early years of our marriage, I actually did the budget and we had a joint account and I used to prorate what I paid on the bills based on our different salaries, and it was never something we discussed; I just did it.

3) Do you feel comfortable with your family and friends knowing that you earn more? Why or why not?

I guess any discomfort is for him, not for [me], because I've worked very hard to get to this point and I've made the sacrifices. In addition, I went back to school to get a second degree. He decided it wasn't worth the time. I choose to go back, then I didn't feel like I should short-change myself. We don't discuss the fact that he didn't go back to school. His personality is different from mine, and so I don't know if additional education would have benefited him. I don't know if he would have aggressively been seeking something [to] commensurate with his education. He is not a risk taker like I am.

4) What feelings do you hide about this relationship dynamic that you can never tell him?

I never discuss my salary with him. He sees my salary only at tax time. He does not ask me about it. It's the elephant in the room. We don't discuss it.

5) What does "head of household" mean to you? Who is the head of the household in your home?

The head of the household is the primary decision maker. In our household it's kind of joint and it rotates based on the situation—who is the best person to handle that situation. Sometimes, since he is the husband, I try to let him take the more traditional position—I try to let him take the lead. He is not always the head of the household; it's kind of a floating position.

If he was the breadwinner I would probably still not defer to him in making the decisions. Because of my personality, I think it depends on who has the best information. I am more detail oriented; he sometimes drops the ball and I have to pick it up and become Miss Fixit. So, things that are important to me or things that can't bear that need a lot of detail in their completion, I go ahead and do.

6) Would you consider leaving your career behind if it was causing your relationship to suffer?

I would not give up my career for my relationship. Even though he doesn't discuss it—it benefits him by me making the additional income.

7) What are your overall expectations of a partner/spouse in a relationship? If those expectations have not been met, what do you think has prevented this?

My expectations are that I would prefer that my husband would be the breadwinner; that he did make a larger income. I feel that I have to make choices to support the family, to live the lifestyle that we both agree we like to live. I can't make the choices I want to make.

At the age I am now, I would like to work part time and be able to cruise into retirement, but I can't afford to do that being the major breadwinner—to reduce my hours or just stop working altogether—even though I have education and experience. I'm not one of those women who would have a problem with not working. I don't have a problem with stopping work. I could still do volunteer work to utilize my education.

He is not a risk-taker and is not able to do the extra to make him the major breadwinner in the family. My bank salary is larger because I have chosen to work part time to reach my financial goals and expectations. I don't feel resentful toward him because I chose to work part time. There were things that I wanted and he couldn't give them to me. I [have] the credentials and experience and initiative to get what I want to get.

8) How similar is your relationship to your parents' relationship? Is that acceptable to you?

My parents had a very traditional relationship. I believe my father did make more than my mother, [but] not by much. My father did work two jobs. I am used to the idea of both parents working. Some of the things I saw with my parents made me so independent. Some things they did well. Other things I saw, I decided I was not going to be that type of wife.

The way my household is running now is the same way my parents' household ran. Initially we handled things jointly but now we have assigned bills, because we handle things differently. I don't even put money into the joint account anymore.

9) Does making more money equate to having more of a voice in the relationship?

I don't think that making more means I have more of a voice, but I make my voice heard. I'm not going to automatically allow him to make decisions independent of me because I'm contributing as much or more into the household. I don't try to take over—there have been situations where I have taken over, but those were situations where I was totally financially responsible.

10) Why did you get married or enter into a long-term relationship?

I got married because, to me, it's the thing to do. I'm very traditional. I know we are probably a minority today because we have been married for decades, and I look around today at people who are single or divorced—and I look at my lifestyle and, for better or for worse, I still feel there's a certain level of security in having a committed mate with you. I like the level of security, of having a committed mate with me. Even though sometimes you feel like you need to be committed. To me, it's the only way to live.

11) If you have children, what type of individual do you want them to marry? Is it different from your relationship and why?

For my daughter, I'm hoping she will marry someone who has financial independence so she won't feel trapped. [She'll] have more choices and not have to live like I'm living. For my son, I hope his career will take off to the point that he can offer that financial security to his wife. I would recommend that my children have that more traditional financial situation with the husband as the breadwinner.

12) Is trust, support, or responsibility a factor in your relationship?

I think support and responsibility are an issue. In general, I feel like some of the things I'm requesting—such as anniversary gifts or things of that nature—I kind of shy away from asking for exactly what I want because of the income difference. I don't want to put him in a financial bind, so I don't say anything. I will just get it for myself.

For things like vacations, I find myself paying for it and later I feel like I didn't even hear him offer to pay for some of it, or pay for a particular event. It's like an expectation that I'm going to be paying when I'm thinking he should have paid for at least part of it.

As far as support, sometimes when I'm putting in hours on my regular job and my part-time job—even little things like getting up in the morning and the bed is not made and I'm busy—I've decided to choose my battles and my chores. If I come home and the bed is not made, then it just doesn't get made, or if the clothes pile up in the basement, I just leave them until I can get to them. So, that's my way of [supporting myself] and not making myself crazy.

In the past, I was always working and taking care of the kids and the house, and yet he [was] always finding time to get to the gym or go see his family. And I said, "What is wrong with this picture?" I am not superwoman. A wise woman said you can't change a person but you can change yourself and people just have to respond to you—so I learned to change myself— and they can respond to me. They can come in and see clothes sitting in the dryer for three days and take them out, or leave them there, it's their choice. But I'm not changing them; they are making the choice.

13) What advice would you give to other women who may be entering a similar arrangement?

I would recommend open communication and conversation. I would discuss expectations upfront regarding it. How comfortable are they with realizing that in order to get what you want you are going to have to support them rather than them supporting you, knowing that when you go on vacation, you will be the one pulling out your credit card versus him. Because it definitely is a different dynamic—typically at a hotel or restaurant the waitress will give the bill to the male—how comfortable are you with that?

14) How has your current dynamic affected your expectations for your spouse and his "role" in the marriage?

I'll try to be as tactful as possible. I have no expectations anymore. The combination of personality, money, and everything else rolled into one, I feel if I expect nothing and I can get something, then it's a bonus. In all fairness, there are things that he does do as far as helping out. I found, over the years, I will get help, but I've found it's not consistent. Unfortunately, the inconsistent part usually occurs when you need him to be consistent, so I've learned to expect nothing.

There is a large salary difference. With my part-time job, my salary is doubles his. Over the years, we have separated our finances, so any issues would be non-financial. His goals in life are not as high as mine are. We don't talk about the fact that I make more. In the past, when he was making more, he would talk about it. But now that I make more, he does not talk about it.

I think there is still the expectation that the man be the breadwinner. I don't as much now as a generation ago. As far as the woman making more, it's often more pressure on the woman to downplay how much she is making, because she is not expected to flaunt that fact, whereas when the man makes more, he can flaunt what he makes and can support his family.

15) *Do you feel the need to overcompensate for the fact that you earn more?*

When we had joint accounts and I was doing the budget, I would prorate the money. If we go out to dinner, before the waiter comes, I might slide him the credit card. Sometimes he does pay for our meals out. He's very neutral about it. It does not seem to bother him.

16) *What do you need from your mate that you are not getting? What do you think your mates needs from you?*

We need to have more discussions. The things that he does independently of me, that affect me, that he will go ahead and do thinking it's OK for me. But I'll have my own financial goals, and with him adding a new financial burden, it affects me. He'll make statements about something he wants to do and then just do it and it has a financial impact. I'm thinking it's in the planning stage and he has already followed through with it. I think he thinks I have more money than I really do.

I think for him, I should keep him more abreast of what I'm doing. My spending and budgeting habits are so different from his, so I guess I should just keep him more informed. I guess I just need to be more open to him. I think he wants more of my time. Between my two jobs and now me wanting to get some more ME time—I probably am not that accessible to him.

I think his goals are being reached but I don't think my goals and aspirations are being met. I need him to be more open about my goals.

Interview #12: Helen

1) When you entered into this relationship, did you know that you would be earning more? What made you comfortable with that? How did your mate feel about this dynamic? How do you feel about this situation now compared to when you entered the relationship?

I have been married twice and currently single. I did not know in the first marriage; I did know in second marriage. In my subsequent relationship now, I knew going in. I got married [the] first time right out of high school—got pregnant. Times were tough. We were living paycheck to paycheck. My husband lost his job. We moved a couple of times. He went through a couple of jobs. I had always worked. My mother always worked. My aunt owned her own business, so I come from a family of independent women. I started a job as a temp and moved up very quickly.

I began earning a lot more money than my husband. My first husband was very insecure. He had a problem [with] that in a very short time. I was making a lot more money than him. He was very suspicious of everything I did. We stayed together for 16 years. I worked hard at trying to keep the marriage together—I wanted to stay together for the children. I look back on it now and think that was crazy. They never saw a loving household.

My second husband had no problem with me earning more money. He was happy just sitting in front of the TV. He did not have any drive, just lived off of me. He was much better for the kids, though. I thought he was making a good living when I met him. I think I perceived that things were better than they really were financially.

We lived together before marriage, so I really knew what the situation was—[that] he was not really a go getter. He was a great housewife as far as cleaning, cooking, shopping. So it did help me a lot. The marriage became sort of a partnership rather than a marriage. I was responsible for everything. If anything broke, it was my responsibility to take care of it—I took care of everything financially. I was completely supporting him, but the marriage lasted 16 years because he was so helpful around the house. He did not have a problem at all with it. It didn't equal happiness because I had a house partner, but I did not have a soul mate.

I wanted to go out and do things, go places, and it got to the point where I was going by myself—he never wanted to go anywhere. I went everywhere alone because he never wanted to go.

2) How does this arrangement with you as the breadwinner make you feel?

I have always been a very responsible person. I always do my best. I have exceeded what my dreams were. I don't have a problem being the major breadwinner. I don't rub it in anybody's face. I was very careful not to bring up that I was the major breadwinner.

3) Do you feel comfortable with your family and friends knowing that you earn more? Why or why not?

I never discussed it with family and friends. We had nice things but I didn't bring it up in my first marriage.

In my second marriage, everyone knew I was the breadwinner. They thought my second husband was using me. I told them that he does things for me—meaning things in the house. I would buy him cars and things, but he was only interested in sports and cars. He wasn't interested in participating in any activities with me. I didn't ask a lot of him. Before we got married he would do things with me, but he stopped once we got married. So, I will never get married again. I don't want anybody else using me.

4) What feelings do you hide about this relationship dynamic that you can never tell him?

In my first marriage, I hid what was going on with the jobs and promotions. I kept that success inside. I didn't share that with him. I downplayed what I did. I got a lot of praise at work, but it didn't translate to home. With the way he was, I knew he would feel like a failure if I shared that with him.

5) *What does "head of household" mean to you? Who is the head of the household in your home?*

Head of household is the person who takes care of the majority of, not only the finances, but just taking care of the activities, planning for the family and the house, getting things fixed, cars, etc. In my first marriage, I was the head of the household, but if anybody asked, I would say that he was. I took care of the checkbook. I would make the decision, but would have him think that he made it. I think male egos work better if you let them take the credit for an idea.

6) *Would you consider leaving your career behind if it was causing your relationship to suffer?*

I would say no, but actually I left two very good careers when I moved out of state with my husband. It was very hard for me to move. We moved because he was in the military. Would I quit my career now? NO.

7) *What are your overall expectations of a partner/spouse in a relationship? If those expectations have not been met, what do you think has prevented this?*

My expectations are just having a partner who loves me completely. I have been very fortunate because even though my first two marriages did not work out, I have finally found my soul mate. He owns his own business. He is independent; he has a lot of friends; he loves to go out; he loves to dance—we love the same music. We see eye to eye. We have so much in common. I love him so much. It's a bond between us and I have finally fallen in love. I can't say that I was truly in love with my first two husbands.

In my current relationship, he supports me in my business, loves me unconditionally, trusts [and] supports me in all my endeavors. We support each other. We enjoy each other. I have been looking for this my whole life. But I'm afraid to get married. When I got married before, the men changed. I think people don't work as hard in a relationship after they get married.

8) How similar is your relationship to your parents' relationship? Is that acceptable to you?

My parents' marriage was very different from mine. My mother always worked, but my father was always the major breadwinner. So I didn't have anything to draw from. I get my strength and independence from her. She is very strong willed.

9) Why did you get married or enter into a long-term relationship?

My first marriage was out of fear. It was a mistake from day one. My mother didn't come to the wedding. My father tried to talk me out of it. I had just graduated high school. I tried to break it off. He was a violent person. He made me feel he was going to kill himself if I didn't marry him. I felt that I would be responsible if he took his life.

He was very controlling. The marriage wasn't all bad. I got two beautiful children from the marriage. My children and I are very close. My daughter is the one who came to me and asked me, "How long are you going to put up with this?" He had a temper—sometimes it was physically violent. It's a shame that I put the kids through that.

My second marriage was for companionship. He was the opposite of my first husband. He was passive and weak. I went from overbearing and violent to someone who was passive and weak. I was not madly in love with him either.

Now I have finally found someone in the middle, someone who can stand on their own two feet, who is independent in his own life. The person I really love. I will never marry again, though.

10) If you have children, what type of individual do you want them to marry? Is it different from your relationship and why?

The concern is not who earns more, but who is on the same level with you mentally. What type of person are they? Do they have your same morals and ideals in a family? Do you have things in common? You need to have some common goals and interests. An active person doesn't match well with a couch potato. It doesn't matter who makes the most money if the husband is comfortable with it—the husband can't be an insecure person.

I don't think income level should be the deciding factor. I don't think a man—in this day and age—should have a problem with a woman making more and if he does, then he is insecure and maybe you should walk away from the relationship.

11) Do you think that more people are satisfied or dissatisfied with this relationship dynamic and why?

I think it's a difficult road to take because there are so many men out there who have the insecurity that they have to be the major breadwinner. And a lot of them have trouble coping with that. As time has gone by, you see less and less of that.

As women have become more educated, getting better positions, I think the tide is turning. In talking to younger people coming up, it's not as much of an issue. You have to go into a relationship as equals. Whether the wife is a homemaker or whatever the roles are. Her contributions are huge as a homemaker. There needs to be an understanding that each is contributing in their own way.

12) Is trust, support, or responsibility a factor in your relationship?

In my first marriage, there was a problem with trust. I was doing nothing, but I was accused of being unfaithful for any small reason—if any man paid any attention to me or if I spoke to someone, even if I smiled at someone he assumed I was having an affair with them. I did trust him. I didn't accuse him of anything.

13) Would you encourage others to have the same relationship dynamic? Why or why not?

I would encourage couples to move forward when the woman earns more if they can handle it. It depends on the person. A lot of it has to do with their education and their upbringing. My son, for example, grew up in a home seeing his mother be a strong person and the wage earner. I think he almost expects that in his wife. He is used to seeing a woman being an equal. It could go the other way. It could be that boys being brought up now, where there is the strong woman at the helm, will expect their spouse to be the same way.

14) What advice would you give to other women who may be entering a similar arrangement?

I would tell the women to be themselves. Let the man see you for who you are. If you love challenges—don't try to hide that. Let them know your goals, ambitions—talk with them. Don't put on an act. They need to be supportive of who you really are.

15) Is there communication within your marriage or is this topic like the elephant in the room?

In my first marriage, it was the elephant in the room. It was never discussed. Second marriage, it was discussed more to the end of the marriage. That was due to my frustration in that he needed to contribute more to the marriage. He had just become too comfortable. I don't mind working hard if I feel I have an equal partner there with me. No matter what it is—just helping me. When I don't see that, then I'm going to have that discussion. You need to step up. "Look, we are all benefitting from what I'm doing. But when I see that you are not contributing—that is not going to work."

16) Does making more money equate to having more of a voice in the relationship?

More income should not affect the voice in the marriage. A housewife should have just as much say. You can't have just one person making all the decisions. You have to sit down and talk about the financial future. You can't have one person who is just spend spend and the other is save save. That marriage is going to crash. You have to both decide that this is what we want for our future.

17) How has your current dynamic affected your expectations for your spouse and his "role" in the marriage?

In the first marriage, no. We pooled our money so he would always pay for it. I would never give him any money or credit card—never ever. In my second marriage, he didn't care. I could pay for anything all the time.

In my current relationship—when we go out for dinner—I can pay or he can pay. It doesn't matter to him. We just take turns paying. He is very secure in who he is. We are pretty equal in what we make.

18) What do you need from your mate that you are not getting? What do you think your mates needs from you?

I always seem to end up with a man who likes cooking. I don't like to cook. I will clean. To this day I don't cook. I will say I did expect him to help me more in the household end of things then I would have if he had been the main wage earner. So you can't be chief breadwinner and top bottle washer, too. It's just a matter of time.

I pretty much insisted that some of the tasks usually relegated to the woman be handled by my husband. When you are tied up in a career, it's very difficult to have three careers and do them simultaneously. You can't do everything 100%. You need to get that spouse to step up and do more. My husbands all cooked and my current mate cooks.

I think my husbands needed more of my time and attention. My career and my childrearing took time away from them.

In my first marriage, I needed acceptance in who I was and I needed him to trust me. Instead, he tried to make me into somebody else. Marriage #2, if he had just put forth some effort—laziness, maybe. He needed to put more into the relationship then what he did. In my current relationship, he works his butt off and I work my butt off, from early in the morning till we go to bed at night. For both of us it's constantly go-go-go. We both thrive on that; it's who we are.

19) What can your mate do to smooth over some of the bumps in the road with regards to salary differences?

I needed support from my mates. If my first husband could have gotten over his own ego enough to support me in who I am and what I was doing, and support the person that I am, we could have had a much happier marriage. In my second marriage, if he had supported me and worked [alongside] me, we could probably still be married today. If you have a woman who is high wage earner, it's probably because you have a stronger will: a Type A personality. It's usually not a blasé type of person. It's what you put into it. Some people just don't have the same drive. That mate needs the support of their spouse. It makes a world of difference.

Interview # 13: Isabelle

1) Did you know you were entering into this type of relationship when you got married?

I did know that I was going to be earning more. And the economy, particularly for [jobs in our state], was very, very different. [My husband] was doing more freelance work and that kind of work kinda dried up as a result of September 11th, because of the nature of the type of work that he was doing. [It was in an industry where] not a lot of companies were trying to have stuff in after September 11th occurred.

2) What made you comfortable with the fact that you made more?

It just wasn't an issue; it was something we had initially talked about, and I knew we had a plan for how we were going to handle expenses. And I should say even though I made slightly more initially, the gap wasn't as big as it is now.

3) How did your husband feel about you making more?

I don't think it was an issue initially for him.

4) How about now?

I think it's less of an issue now, but it has been an issue over the course of our marriage. It has caused some problems.

5) How about you? Do you feel it's more of an issue with you now?

That's a good question. I am actually not working full time. I'm doing more freelance work, and even with the combination of my freelance work, I have some other money coming in. I still manage to be in a position where I'm still making a little bit more. I still have some of the same financial responsibility even though I'm not working full time. So I'm hoping some of those things will shift, as I am not working as consistently as I have been in the past.

6) How does the arrangement with you being the breadwinner make you feel?

Sometimes [I feel like] it bothers me. There are things that I feel like I want do, and I recognize that I am not going to wait for my husband to treat me to a five-star restaurant. If I want to go to the newest, latest, hottest, I will have to more than likely bite the bullet and pay for it myself. Sometimes I do have a measure of, I don't know if regret is the right word, but I sometimes think it would be nice to be treated, and I guess I have to alter my perception of what being treated means, recognizing that the way that he will treat me is going to be different based on what he is able to do.

7) Do you feel comfortable about your friends and family knowing that you earn more?

I thinks it's a given. I think that there is a perception when you work for a company like [mine]—you have high earning potential, or stock, regardless of whether or not that's the case. And I think even now it's funny. I was at a family gathering —[a family member commented that I have money]. She doesn't know anything about how much money I make, even though I am no longer with [my company] people still think there is stock or other money—in that I probably have some money somewhere.

8) Are you OK with your family knowing that you make more? Do you feel like you have to hide it or cover it up?

Fundamentally, I'm a frugal person. By nature I like certain things, like going out for a nice dinner once in a while. We do take trips once in a while—usually once a year—but I think, fundamentally, I'm going to WalMart, so most of what people think is a perception not reality.

9) What about his family? Is he comfortable with them knowing?

I'm not sure what they think. I'm not sure, but I think there is an assumption. I don't know if he has shared that I make more. I'm sure that they have the perception that I'm the breadwinner.

10) No kick back from family; no snide remarks like he's using you [or] you're supporting him?

Because, it's not like he's not bringing anything to the table, like he's not watching Jerry Springer or anything while I'm working, whether it's in the office or doing my side hustle. That's not really the case, so I don't feel that there has been any kick back or snide remarks.

12) *What do you hide about your feelings, about this relationship dynamic, that you can never tell him?*

Well, the big thing is wanting to be treated every once in a while. Wanting to go to a [fancy] restaurant and not having to worry about paying for it. Even though I'm being transparent, I think it would make him feel less than. Somehow I think he would perceive it very differently than the intended message.

13) *What does head of household mean to you and who do you think is the head of your household?*

I would say, for all intents and purposes, I'm the head of the household because I carry the brunt of the financial household expenses and the house is in my name. That was a sore point of contention for my husband, at least initially.

But I remember when we were getting the house, my realtor said, 'You can get everything yourself," and his credit would have hurt us, so the advice was to do everything myself. The house is in my name and pretty much everything else, except [gas and electric] and maybe one or two other bills are his, but the rest of them fall under my responsibility. We do have a fund where we share. It's not like I'm paying all of the mortgage by myself. When it came to the down payment and closing cost, that fell on my shoulders.

[Head of household is] the person who is really responsible for the financial aspect of the household expenses. Making sure the bills are paid, carrying the brunt of the financial responsibilities, keeping a roof over our head and food on the table; the mortgage is taken care of.

14) What about decision making? Do you find you take on that role as well? Who has the final say?

I don't look at head of household as being my way or the highway. That's not my perspective at all. I think we share in the decision making in the house. So, for me, it's not, "Because I pay this, it's gonna be what I say." When it comes time to do certain things, we share in the decision making, whether it's cutting down on a bill or going with a different provider for lawn service—I'm still having those conversations with him.

15) You're comfortable with having an equal say in decisions. It's not you don't feel that as a man he should be making the final decision.

All things being considered when it comes to household decisions, we are equal. I'm comfortable with that.

16) Would you consider leaving your career behind if it's causing your relationship to suffer?

No. One of the reasons I left my job [was] because of the needs of my parents rather than my mate. Ironically, the reason I left my job was because my mother became ill and was hospitalized. She previously handled the business of their household and my father needed help, so I had to take over the management of their household. [I] didn't see that my job caused a problem in my marriage.

17) [What if your] husband was to say, "You making more is making me feel like less of a man. I need you to cut back"?

I would need to understand why the dynamic was shifting because it was a part of the relationship from the beginning. Why, now, is it a problem when it hasn't been throughout [the] history of our relationship?

18) Expectations of spouse?

Emotional support, financial support (even though I'm considered to be the breadwinner), at least a balance as well, sex, companionship, an active role raising children (even we don't have them yet). For me, since my older parents have needs, when I have to travel, I need for him to check on my parents because they are his parents too, now. I need you to check on my mother at least once or twice if I'm gone for a week.

19) How similar is your relationship to your parents?

My parents were more equal—my father made more when he was working—so very different. But in spite of the fact that my father was the breadwinner, he depended on my mother a lot, and now me, for helping with household expenditure.

20) Is it accepted that your marriage is different? Do you feel resentful, like a fish out of water?

For me, the model of relationships had very little to do with finances. I didn't understand what their financial situation was like until I was much older. When I think about what their relationship was for me as a model, I think more about the companionship, the just being there, having a loving relationship and recognizing what that looks like rather than the financial component.

21) Why did you get married or enter into a long-term relationship?

I never thought I was going to get married. I just always felt like I was meant to be single. My husband was my good friend —really, really good friends all throughout school, and maintained a relationship after. Honestly, when I think about why I said "yes," it was because he loved me the way I needed to be loved.

22) Do you think that more people are satisfied or dissatisfied with this relationship dynamic and why?

I don't know the financial dynamics of my friend's relationships. I don't know who is the higher earner. I know my close girlfriend who is going through a divorce now. I think she and her husband earned the same thing, so I don't think they were more satisfied because they made the same thing.

23) Is trust, support, or responsibility a factor in your relationship?

I think trust is an issue. I feel supported; I feel like my husband has a responsibility, but I think with any type of relationship, when you have to force yourself to become vulnerable, there concern: do you deserve this? When you have to compromise, I think you have to have trust. It takes time. Trust is always something growing and developing.

24) Would you encourage others to have the same relationship dynamic? Why or why not?

It depends upon what you are looking for. If you are the type of woman who is looking for a husband to financially support you, then obviously no. But if you are looking for emotional support, companionship, friendship, then I don't see too much of an issue. It's important to figure out how to make that work for you. If you are strong and are looking for more of the softer things, than getting married for financial support, then I don't see a problem with it.

25) In your experience most of the wives are making more?

For most of my friends, the couples are equal or probably the wives are making more. I'm only saying that because most of my friends have more education than their husbands. I can only assume that the wives are making more because they have more education. For example, I have a Master's degree and my husband has a Bachelor's degree.

26) What advice would you give to other women who may be entering a similar arrangement?

You have to have a conversation about how you are going to divide the finances. A lot of marriages end not so much for infidelity but due to financial situations that arise. It's not a sexy conversation, not romantic. If you don't have the conversation about who is going to be responsible for what, then resentment can enter into the relationship. To avoid that, it's important to really, really have the talk up front.

I think we have the same perspective in terms of what we want for ourselves as a family. We are not financially equally yoked, but we are in every other aspect.

27) Is there communication within your marriage or is this topic like the elephant in the room?

No. We always have this conversation—like when we are out for dinner. We had the talk when I knew I was not going to be working full time anymore. How are we [going to] handle situation XYZ. We were in a kind of romantic setting. We talked about if we paid some bills now he would have more to contribute, more on a monthly basis to the household. We talk about it regularly.

28) Decisions in the household: Should woman who is the higher earner have more or at least an equal say than housewives?

What you make should not be determined your voice. Housewives do a lot, even [when] they aren't earning income at a regular job. Decisions should be made together. When we talked about going on vacations, we talked about what we each want to do. We probably are very unique in that we over-communicate about some things. I like to check and recheck. I'll say, "This is what I said, now what did you hear?" I recognize that our brains are different and we process information differently. Men are not great communicators. A lot of times my husband will think he communicated something to me and I'm like, "That [is] not what I heard." So, we'll go back and review the conversation and kind of say, "OK, we could have said this differently." I think communication is the most important element in any marriage—whether it's about finances or the school for kids or where [are] you going to live. It [is] definitely difficult.

29) Do you feel the need to overcompensate?

No. The conversation will take place before we go out: "How are we gonna handle this? Am I paying this?" So, I feel like we are already talking about it. I have a friend—another couple we go out with—I don't know who makes the most money, but I know she always pays the bill. So, I don't know if that's the card they use for those types of expenses or what, but I just don't feel like it's a real serious issue. I don't feel like I need to make sure [.....] has money to pay the bill. It's not something I think about.

30) How has it affected your expectation in the marriage?

I think it's the Cinderella complex, where we, as women, are conditioned to think that men are supposed to provide for us in a certain way. Whether it's realistic or not, unfortunately all the story books and our [own] conditioning tells us this is how [it] is supposed to be, and so when I think about the dynamics in my own relations, I do kinda wish that my husband could treat me. And he does, but those instances are few and far between, so it's kind of a paradigm shift for what we think we are supposed to have as far as the reality of what marriage is really like.

31) Should the husband assume the role of wage earner? Should he have other roles he should assume?

My first response is no. It's not like he's home every day. I'm the one who is at home [working during the day]. I don't expect him to do five loads of clothes and the house to be vacuumed just because I make more money. My perspective is a little skewed anyway, because my father is a lot older than my mother, and he retired when my mother still worked. Because of that, I think men should play equal roles in the household, period. In terms of cooking dinner, my father cooked dinner, packed our lunch, went on school trips, because he was retired and my mother was still working.

So, if I look at it from a role perspective, I would say, "OK, there is something wrong with this picture," but in reality, understanding that he was a house husband because he retired young. My mother was still young; I grew up seeing that: OK, men do this, too. So, my expectations are different because of the way I was raised. If I go away, I don't expect things to be piled up at the front door. My husband probably does a marathon cleanup before I return anyway, but in general, I'll be out and call home and say, "What's for dinner?" That's how I was raised.

32) What do you need that you are not getting?

Better communication. Even though I feel like I over-communicate, I don't think he does the same. Or, when he does communicate, he needs to check back with me to make sure that I have received the information the same way: "Did you understand I meant this?" A lot of times I received it in a totally different way, kind of doing that check. It's like a joke now. I said, "So and so, did you get that," and he'll say, "Check." We've had some instances when I feel like we were on two different levels and he said, "We talked about this," and I said, "No, that's not how the conversation went; that's not what I remember."

Example: When we had a conversation about what bills could be tackled while I'm doing the freelance thing—and he had more of a steady income—he said he wanted to pay off [some debt]. In my mind, I don't remember him saying a number of what he owed, just, "Let's get some of these bills paid," so he could contribute more to the household. We were working on getting the bills eliminated, so I don't think a dollar amount was ever quoted. When he came back to me and said [what he owed], I looked at him like he had grown a second head, "I don't ever remember you telling me any number." I'm thinking about maybe [a few] thousand. He said, "I told you." I said, "NOPE, we didn't have that conversation. We did talk about eliminating these bills but never did I hear [that much]." So, that's an example of a conversation like that where I clearly remember the conversation, but the dollar amount was not clearly communicated.

The big key was you'll be able to contribute more to the household but the dollar amount was not conveyed clearly. He'll send me an instant message or text. I don't count that as communication for important conversations.

33) What do you think your mate needs from you that he's not getting?

More of my time and for me to be more present. Today is a perfect example. I'm home during the day; I'm going to run errands. He won't get home till after nine o'clock. I won't be getting home until the same time as him tonight or following him. I was sleep when he left this morning, so we will have gone the whole day without seeing each other. I haven't talked to him on the phone at all today, but then in the evenings—for example, last night I didn't get home until after 10:00 p.m. I think the game was on, so we were both on the computer in the same room. I logged in to check email. I think we are both guilty of this. I will say, "Put your phone down; shut the computer down; and let's talk or watch a movie." That's why we have so many conversations over dinner, because there are so many distractions at home.

Monday is a day when I'm not leaving out the door. It's [a holiday] and I just want to spend the day together. [It] is very rare that we do that. It's important that on Monday we spend the day together. I know there may be some conversations when I'm sending an email, when I may not have not processed all of the conversation, so that's why we started with, "OK, did you understand what I said?" Check.

34) What is the final message for what your mate can do to make it easier for you?

Obviously, when you have this type of situation, you say, "What is feasible? What makes sense? What's fair?" So, we can pay the bills we have so we can do what we need to do, and have some money so we can do what we want to do. I think for me, if there are months when you are falling short, you need to communicate with me before the day [the bill is] due or is past due. Advance communication on who is going to be responsible for what. So, if I have to pick up the slack, I need to know in advance so there is no strain in other areas.

Chapter Four
A Good Leader is Hard to Find

Men, Please Read!

CONTRARY TO WHAT SOME MEN may believe, most professional women in a marriage *want* the man to lead! There is a part of her that wants to submit to a certain type of man. A common misconception in popular culture is that a successful career woman "doesn't need a man." But that is simply not true. She does indeed need him, but desires a responsible mate who knows how to be a proficient leader. The difference between the high-earning wife of today and the dependent wife of yesteryear is that the breadwinning wife has a choice of whether to submit or not. Female breadwinners no longer need to barter their subservience and docility for the financial security of a marriage.

The days when the presence of a Y chromosome gave a man the inherent right to lead are disappearing right before our eyes. Traditionally, men have felt entitled to lead because of the perceived omnipotence of the male gender, combined, perhaps, with greater education, greater intelligence, or more worldly life experiences. But a man who falls in love with a driven female breadwinner needs to recognize that leadership in her world has to be earned. She witnessed the ascension of leaders in academia and corporate America only after hard work and appropriate skills were exhibited. So, it is difficult for her to expect anything less than those attributes from the leader in her marriage. Through educational **pursuits and career advancement, she has proven that she** is quite an effective leader in her own right. She is expecting **that her husband will enhance her life with** *proficient* **leader**ship and unconditional love.

If a wife of the 1940s attracted and married a husband **without proper leadership skills, she would have no choice** but to suffer. She would have begrudgingly endured that situation with little power to change it. A wife during that **era would not have felt empowered enough to expect more** from her mate. American history has shown that before the **1960s, women were very dependent on their spouses for** countless aspects of their existence. They couldn't drive; they didn't know how to write checks; they couldn't apply for credit in their own name; they couldn't fly alone on some **airlines; they were uncomfortable traveling the streets alone as they were barred from certain establishments because of** their gender. This created an almost infantile dependence on their male counterparts. Without a source of income to sustain herself or her children, this more traditional wife would **have lacked bargaining power, leaving her feeling disempow**ered and trapped in that marriage. Contrarily, a woman with education and income ultimately has more leverage in her relationship. If necessary, these women have the confidence, education, life experiences, and training to provide leadership for the household if her husband fails to deliver.

To describe the importance of an efficient leader in a marriage, let's use the rhythmic exchange of Salsa dancing as a metaphor. A man MUST lead in this style of dance; otherwise, the couple risks appearing disorganized and inexperienced on the dance floor. If the male dancer fails to lead

A Good Leader is Hard to Find | 161

his partner effectively, the female will respond in one of two ways. Some women will simply walk away out of frustration and embarrassment. Or in the case of a more experienced **female dancer,** *she* will be forced to take the lead, initiating **her own moves, spins, and dips! She will not wait for him to** figure it out, nor will she follow a partner who is ineffectively "attempting" to lead her through the dance. Either he will **lead, or she will take over as his leader!**

If a female breadwinner recognizes that her husband lacks the ability to lead, she will be forced to "grow one" and **take over! This is a very important point that men married to** educated, high-achieving women must understand. Although **you may not be able to see it, your wife does indeed have** a "penis!" This metaphor is apologetically graphic, but it is easier to explain this concept in blatant terms. Husbands of **female breadwinners are probably unaware that their wives** have a "penis" and that it has helped her to succeed in competitive academic and workplace environments. Terms like "dog-eat-dog world" and James Brown's "It's a Man's World" describe the caustic environment that she has had to endure in order to succeed. The husbands of female breadwinners must recognize that at some point in her life, his lovely wife has had to trade in her pantyhose for a jock strap! She *needed* a "penis" to get to where she is today, particularly if she is at the top of the food chain in education or career.

When I say that your wife has a "penis," I am, of course, speaking in a figurative sense. What I mean is that she has had to assume very masculine characteristics to assimilate and succeed in male-dominated environments. She has had **to act tough like a man, shedding some of her more feminine** and nurturing characteristics, while in the physical space of her workplace. This masculine persona is not something that she necessarily enjoys but is merely an adaptation to what she sees around her. She has witnessed that "male" behavior patterns get rewarded with advancement. She has had to act accordingly to get where she wants to be. Along her path to success, **female breadwinners have undoubtedly faced many** obstacles including discrimination which may have stemmed from sexism, classism, racism, ageism, or a combination of these. She has an inherent fire within her that compels her to succeed. This fire is not easily quenched, not even after saying "I do" and committing herself to you as her husband. So **while she is devoted to you in spirit, there is a part of her that** has had to fight like a junkyard dog to get to where she is in life. And this part of her (her "penis") is not easily put to rest.

As a collective, female breadwinners of today possess greater intellect, ambition, and life experiences than any cohort of females throughout American history. But men who assume that female breadwinners want to lead and "wear the pants" in the marriage are misinformed. She leads out of *necessity*, not desire! If she is placed in a position to have to **take over due to absent leadership in the marriage, she may** feel resentful. Most of these women hate being forced into "rescue mode." Some women may interpret a lack of leadership from their mates as a sign of weakness. After all, she still desires to see her husband act as the "knight in shining armor"—the stuff that little girl's dreams are made of.

For example, let's think of a scenario in which there is an imaginary kingdom lead by a king. This king has a multitude of subjects. The strength of leadership that the king displays will have a lot to do with how well his subjects respect him and heed his rulings. If the king shows that he is competent as a leader, his subjects will be loyal and follow. On the other hand, if the king shows a lack of responsibility and direction for the kingdom, his subjects will lose faith in his leadership. They will heed his rulings less avidly and, over time, a coup may likely occur. This imaginary kingdom is an appropriate metaphor by which to measure the functioning of the common household. If a wife sees no leadership, her tendency to heed her husband's desires will lessen over time and she may eventually try to take over. Again, this reaction is born **out of necessity, not desire! This brewing power struggle will** ultimately lead to bigger problems over the course of the marriage.

Although she is a brave woman, when she committed **herself to you through marriage, she became extremely** afraid. She is afraid of handing off every aspect of her life **over to YOU—something that her counterparts of the male** gender would never be asked to do. She is placing a *tremendous* **amount of trust in you and your ability to take care of** her. And for that reason, her expectations of you in the relationship may subconsciously change immediately after you both say, "I do." If she witnessed you pay a bill late during the courtship period, she can blow it off as, "It's a bad habit but, hey, that's his credit score not mine." She may have witnessed you forgetting to take out the trash or neglecting to fix a broken window in your bachelor pad. But if she loves **you and loves other things about you, then she will excuse** these shortcomings. She will say to herself, "Well, that's his apartment in shambles, not mine. He's a good man with a lot of good qualities. Who cares if he forgets to change a light bulb?"

But after you two share wedding vows, begin sharing a **living space, and you as the man become the head of household**—all of those small shortcomings suddenly become MAJOR to her. Because now you are the captain of her ship and, ultimately, you are in control of her destiny and happiness moving forward. This realization is frightening for a woman who has proven herself to be driven, assertive, and successful. When she sees a burned out light bulb that sits unaddressed for two weeks, she may interpret this as "Hmm... why isn't he taking care of our household? Isn't that what a real leader does?" And when every other man on your street can have his trashcan at the curbside on time, but she sees **you fumbling to get yours there before the trash truck pulls** away, she becomes afraid. She is afraid that maybe she was mistaken. Maybe you are not equipped to be the captain of **her ship—and every woman feels that** *her* **ship is the most** precious vessel on all of the high seas.

The female breadwinner feels empowered and capable and wants to see her husband's qualities match or exceed her own. When a husband's missed opportunities to lead compound over years of a marriage, a funny thing happens. That "penis" that she needed to get through college or law school, or graduate school or medical school, or corporate America, may begin to regain nerve endings. The high-earning woman, unlike the housewife of yesteryear, has a choice. She can *choose* to leave that "penis" tucked away for the life of your marriage OR she can rely on it once again when her household seems to be falling apart around her. The high-earning **and high-achieving woman will NEVER let her vessel sink like** the Titanic. She may have handed you the reins of her destiny **on your wedding day, but she will take them right back if she** finds that you are incapable of being an effective captain.

There are some men who are honestly unaware of their wife's expectations for him to lead, because the couple has never engaged in an honest discussion. In other marriages, **the husband may have displayed more leadership** *prior* **to her** acquiring breadwinner status. But these qualities may have lapsed for many reasons. Husbands of female breadwinners **are faced with unique challenges to their ego and self-es**teem. In addition to disparities in education as the root cause **behind the rise of female breadwinners, there are many other untoward circumstances that may have contributed to her** income surpassing his. These include job loss, under-employment after the recession, a relinquishment of his occupation to support her career, retirement, chronic illness, disability, to name a few. As a result of such complex and life-changing events, some husbands can suffer from low self-esteem, un**diagnosed depression, substance abuse, and an overall sense** of hopelessness. Such challenges may contribute to a lapse in his leadership efforts for a period or a cessation altogether. Female breadwinners need to be sensitive as their husbands react to life circumstances that would be difficult for anyone to handle. She needs to support him and reassure him that he is still important, needed, and desired as her mate. She needs him to understand that no matter who makes what income—he can still be the leader of the pack!

It is not an uncommon practice in our society to associate money with power. In the minds of some men, if the woman has the money, then she has the power, right? WRONG!! **This is a backwards way to interpret this unique dynamic of a** higher-earning female in a marriage. Men, please don't relin**quish your role as leader simply because her earned income** surpasses yours. You should maintain your place as head of the household, but you may have to modify your behavior while redefining your position.

Different men handle change in different ways. Here is an example. Imagine a scenario in which a man was previously able-bodied. Due to some horrible circumstance, he is faced with a horrible new reality of being a paraplegic and is sitting in the middle of the floor. He is then asked to find a way to get from where he is sitting to another place, point B. There will be a subset of men who will get creative by lifting their torsos using the strength of their arms, and walking on their hands from point A to point B. Another subset will lay their bodies flat and roll their torso from point A to point B. And a third subset of these men will respond angrily and tearfully by saying, "Without any legs, it's impossible for me to get from point A to point B!" This third group of men has failed to redefine themselves within the context of their new reality, which in this hypothetical scenario happens to be a disability. Unfortunately, this subset of men feel that their mobility is defined by the presence of legs, which they no longer have.

If we extrapolate from this example to the husbands of female breadwinners, similarities may become evident. If some husbands feel that they have lost the ability to "bring home the bacon," they may feel as if they've lost their purpose as a husband. They may fail to comprehend another avenue through which they can be relevant to their wives and families. They have missed an opportunity to redefine themselves within the context of their new reality. In a state of desperation, some husbands throw their hands in the air and relinquish their position as head of household. They may even *assume* that this is what their wives want from them. Clarification: This is NOT what your wife wants from you!

Men should instead re-invent themselves. Be creative; think **outside the box to provide for your family in a manner that supersedes dollars and cents!**

So what type of leadership does the female breadwinner desire? Or, said another way, what is the "love language" that will persuade such a woman to submit. Thus, allowing a husband to claim his position as the traditional "head of household." The "love language" to which this unique category of woman responds is not a language in a literal sense. Instead, it is an effective, non-verbal form of communication that will convince her that he is prepared to lead: HIS ACTIONS! This **style of leadership has much less to do with spoken feelings,** promises, or emotions. Instead, it has everything to do with **how a husband behaves and how much he is willing to sacrifice** to be the best leader for the family. So what sort of ACTIONS does the female breadwinner desire to see in her **leader? Well, there are several ways that a man can excel at** being a leader—probably more ways than I can name. But I will mention four qualities that, in my opinion, top the list. If a man focuses on these four characteristics, he can easily persuade his wife to fall in line: financial literacy, fairness, respect, and sacrifice. Because of the importance of these concepts, each will be revisited separately in later chapters.

Let's start with financial literacy. That means that she is looking to you to provide financial guidance for the household. While I understand that money is not everything, that **cliché is usually perpetuated by those that** *have* **money as** opposed to those that don't! Providing financial direction and creating wealth provides security for the household and increases the family's options for the future. Many husbands may come into the marriage with an adept affinity for financial literacy. That places them in front of the eight ball. But **what about those men who lack the knowledge to carve out** a financial direction for his family? Some husbands may have **lacked proper training in money management during adoles**-cence or life's experiences. Even if a husband is not innately **frugal, or has no good sense of bookkeeping or balancing** checkbooks, it is not hard to learn some basics. Paying bills on time (thus preserving credit worthiness), saving for emergencies, investing for college, and preparing for retirement are the basic tenets of financial literacy. And while this list may seem daunting, it really only takes one meeting with a financial advisor to get on the right track. If he would rather not pay a financial advisor, he can research options online, purchase a personal finance manual, or receive advice from friends/colleagues who are financially successful.

By financial literacy, I really just mean taking the initiative to prepare your family financially for the future. With these easy steps, you can provide a sound direction for your family; and over time you will have increased your family's wealth. Even if there are times when you are only putting away peanuts due to a strapped financial situation, you are still displaying the qualities of discipline and financial know-how. These are undeniable qualities of an effective leader.

Another example of qualities desired by female breadwinners is fairness. This sounds simple enough, since we all remember being taught that "fairness is a virtue" as a toddler in the sandbox. But fairness takes on a new dimension for a female breadwinner within the context of a marriage. **In a nutshell, fairness to a female breadwinner means that gender-based assignments or tasks become null and void** when it comes to the successful running of the household. A leader ensures that his household runs in an orderly fashion, regardless of who is completing the tasks that are keeping it in running order.

Let's face it. We have entered a new millennium and the world is moving toward a new equilibrium in gender relations. This is particularly true with regards to marital roles and expectations. Outdated assumptions about "male" or "female" duties in the marriage need to be cast aside. Female breadwinners, regardless of the reason, have had to assume a MAJOR responsibility in the marriage that was traditionally considered to be a "male" duty (i.e. the breadwinner). So, in all FAIRNESS, her husband should return the favor by assuming duties that are traditionally "female" to balance things out. This is not a "tit-for-tat" sort of request. This desire has more to do with the logistics of work-related time constraints that female breadwinners must endure. Breadwinning wives cannot do it all! When these wives return from a hard-days' work, it is illogical for her to have to cook, clean, rear the children, pay the bills, and still have enough energy to act as a sexual concubine! I am not implying that the husband must suddenly take over the lion's share of household duties, simply because his income was surpassed. That could be interpreted as a punishment or a demotion. What I am suggesting is a JOINT EFFORT! Teamwork and fairness are tenets of a successful marriage. Let's shed those archaic and closed-minded limitations regarding which chores belong to which gender. Rather than engaging in a gender struggle over chores, a leader's energy is much better spent filling in the gaps and ensuring that the household is productive and functioning efficiently. Both partners in the marriage must feel a balance in their contributions to achieve this end.

The next quality that female breadwinners desire in their leaders is respect. Showing respect to others is the currency with which leaders achieve results. By this I mean that in order **for a leader to be successful, he has to have a support** staff that heeds his instruction. Showing respect to his supporters is an effective way for a leader to preserve their loyalty and support. We are all privy to the fact that the manner in which a message is delivered is just as important as the message itself. A female breadwinner may be more sensitive than a traditional wife regarding the way her husband treats her and speaks to her when exercising his leadership. These **women may be accustomed to having power and authority in** the workplace; that setting may include the hospital, courtroom, or boardroom. She is used to being respected and having her demands heeded by surrounding staff. So, how do **you think she will respond when she arrives home to you,** her mate, and is made to feel like one of your lowly subjects?

It is important for husbands to realize that their wife's success in education or career should warrant some degree of respect. The same way she is respected at work, she will **want to feel respected at home by the man that she loves** and to whom she has committed her life. Celebrate her ac**complishments; and in doing so, acknowledge her as the** intelligent and capable individual that she has become. She does not want to be made to feel that she is "just a dame" or consistently treated like a subordinate. She despises a condescending approach in your treatment toward her. Your female breadwinner has a lot to offer as your helpmeet and partner. As the head of household, don't expect her to go "sit in the corner and look pretty" when challenges arise—whether it's a busted pipe or a financial setback. Allow her to contribute the talents that she has garnered over her career including troubleshooting, problem solving, conflict resolution, negotiation, and multi-tasking. If you respect her opinion and accept her support, her ability to enhance your leadership will be boundless!

The last quality contributing to sound leadership is sacrifice. This one is MAJOR! Female breadwinners want to see evidence of the fact that her husband will put the needs of the family before his own. She feels that no matter what effort she is putting forth, he is to put forth even more. For example, if the household is trying to save for a specific financial goal, a leader who exhibits sacrifice by eating peanut butter and jelly sandwiches instead of buying lunch at work is setting an excellent example for the entire family. Through his actions, he has shown his family that he is serious about the task at hand. He has shown that he is willing to do whatever it takes to accomplish that goal for the family. If the family is experiencing financial difficulty, a leader may exhibit sacrifice by finding a second job or a source of side income. Sacrifice means taking on the lion's share of whatever burdens the family must endure. Sacrifice is the absence of self-centeredness and the need to impress others. It is a reassuring feeling for a female breadwinner to know that her husband will forfeit his own comfort or well-being to protect his wife and family. A leader's ACTIONS should raise the standards and expectations of the entire household, and will ultimately reinforce the admiration bestowed upon him. Husbands, your wife and children are watching and they will subconsciously mimic the level of dedication displayed by you as the leader.

Proficient leadership is of *paramount* importance to a female breadwinner. She desires a leader who uses actions instead of words to provide an overall direction for the family—ultimately moving them toward a place of greater happiness, order, wealth, and fulfillment. Despite feelings of empowerment in her career, a part of her is still waiting on that "knight in shining armor" that she dreamed of as a young girl. **The leader she desires understands the magnitude and** significance of his position, and rebukes feeling of entitlement based on gender. The majority of female breadwinners will defer to their husbands in the establishment of the "head of household" in the marriage. Men should understand that **she does not *want*** this role, but she will fill this position by default in the circumstance of poor leadership. Despite any differences in salary, the husband of a female breadwinner should redefine himself, reinvent himself, and regain purpose as the provider of much more than just money. By demonstrating financial literacy, fairness, respect, and sacrifice, a **husband can convince his wife that he is indeed the leader of** which dreams are made.

Chapter Five
I Swear to Tell the Whole Truth and Nothing but Half the Truth!

ALTHOUGH OUR SOCIETY AS A whole is more accepting of equality between the sexes, marriages containing a female breadwinner remain shrouded in secrecy and shame. Women decline to discuss it with friends and family for fear of emasculating their husbands. Most men refuse to reveal this dynamic to their confidants for fear of being perceived as less of a man. This pattern of withholding and lack of communication doesn't just apply to the sharing with those *outside* the marriage. Testimonies revealed in this book suggest that many married couples experiencing this dynamic won't even communicate honestly with their own partner! This can create a very alienating and detached existence for both husband and wife. The women interviewed for this book can attest that their status as breadwinner is the proverbial "elephant in the room" within their relationships. So, how do we as a society address each gender's honest feelings, reservations, and desires if both men and women are afraid to even discuss it?

Communication is pivotal to ensuring the survival of any relationship, platonic or romantic. Unfortunately, many female breadwinners refrain from fully communicating how this dynamic of being the breadwinner makes them feel. Thanks to a strong maternal instinct, most wives are naturally protective of their husbands and families. Female breadwinners, as a unique group of wives, can be even more fiercely protective of their husband's ego and the way he is perceived in society. There are times when she may feel guilty that she has placed her husband in a position that makes him feel emasculated. I am not saying that her thought process is valid by any means. Rationality aside, she may harbor the sentiment that this seemingly backwards dynamic in her relationship is **her fault! She may feel responsible for feelings of inadequacy or shame that her husband may experience at the hands of** the outside world. That is, if he measures himself by age-old standards and traditions.

So, you can imagine how difficult it may be for a female **breadwinner to express some very important truths regarding what she may need in the marriage that she is not getting.** Some of these wives may be relentlessly fearful that the honest truth will crush her husband's ego. The last thing she wants to do is add to any sense of insufficiency that he may encounter in the marriage and outside the home. Her natural instinct is to protect him like a mother bear protecting her cub. You will hear some say that a man's ego can never recover from some forms of damage, particularly those initiated by a person he loves and respects. A man's ego—his bravado, his machismo, his mojo—can be a huge part of his identity as a person.

Whether accurate or not, the term "ego" is predomi**nantly described as component of the psychic apparatus of the** *male* gender. The term ego is less frequently ascribed to those of the female gender. This may imply that females wrestle less with the concept of "ego" as a component of their existence. As a result, women may fail to fully understand this amorphous concept. They struggle in processing their husband's ego and how to work around it for the betterment of the marriage. The less she understands about this concept of male ego, the more she fears it.

So, how does one go about sharing potentially hurtful thoughts like, "I am resentful because I can't be a stay-at-home mom like the other ladies on our street," or, "It's hard for me to heed your direction as the head of household because I have more education and life experiences than you; help me to work through this dilemma"? Such thoughts that higher-earning women hide could completely shatter a husband's ego, which may never recover. If she does take the **risk of complete honesty, his bruised ego can manifest itself** through infidelity (seeking validation outside the marriage), emotional withdrawal, and resentment. These hurt feelings fester over time and can eventually ruin a marriage, particularly if his feelings go unrecognized and unresolved.

The sad result is that many of the thoughts and feelings that female breadwinners hide will NEVER be shared. This pattern of withholding is unhealthy to a marriage. Some of **these issues may be in the forefront of her consciousness and** may be directly affecting her ability to achieve happiness in this union. But the breadwinner may feel that her husband is not strong enough to handle the truth. What does she do?

As nurturers, many women display a natural tendency to place their needs aside to cater to the needs of others. Un**fortunately, such altruism can result in the needs of female** breadwinners being overlooked and ignored in the marriage. If she has negative feelings about her circumstance as the breadwinner and they are left unaddressed, they can begin to fester and can contribute to the deterioration of the marriage.

This pattern of prioritizing her husband's ego over her own happiness can be a challenge for any woman. I am not **implying that this is the appropriate approach for female** breadwinners. I am simply admitting that this pattern of behavior does exist. This tactic requires extreme patience and restraint and can prove to be emotionally taxing over time. **Breadwinner Brenda hints to the challenges of such behavior:** "I think in trying not to emasculate the husband, sometimes women in these relationships stuff some of their feelings in the closet—right or wrong. There are times when you just have to swallow it and go on. It's a sacrifice that I've chosen to make. I hope I'll choose to make it forever and ever, but I can see how you might not want to do it forever. It's hard."

A healthy marriage requires each partner's needs to be acknowledged and addressed. This self-inflicted one-sided approach that some female breadwinners practice may not be sustainable over years of marriage. Ultimately, feelings of resentment may develop under the surface.

Some female breadwinners recognize that their husband's ego or worth is intimately tied to his career accomplishments and financial success. Her position as the bread**winner may be a constant source of shame for him as a man** and as a husband. As a result, some wives will downplay or **hide career details and accomplishments to avoid feeling** that they are throwing salt in a wound. Monica admitted: "He could not tell you anything about what I do pertaining **to my career advancements or much of anything about m**y job. I just withhold that information. I just don't share my successes with him." To Monica, withholding important information about her successful career is her emotional band-aid of choice.

Some husbands of female breadwinners associate money with power, believing that he (or she) who makes the most money rules the roost. If a woman recognizes that her mate holds fast to this belief, should she still reveal her high salary? **Should she give it to him straight, no chaser, and endure** the inevitable emotional fall-out? Or, should she simply refrain from sharing? Gina chose the latter in her marriage: "I never discuss my salary with him. He sees my salary only at tax time. He does not ask me about it. It's the elephant in the room." Some people believe that the withholding of information is just another form of lying. When has lying ever been a healthy means to an end in a relationship? Whether healthy or not, it is a common form of placation practiced by female breadwinners as they attempt to relate to their mates within the context of a difficult circumstance.

The goals of this book are varied. The first goal is to convince female breadwinners to set aside their protective instincts long enough to recognize what they need to survive. **I implore this unique category of wife to engage in an exer**cise of self-exploration and introspection. Sadly, most of the **women I interviewed for this book stated that** my interview was the first time they had ever verbalized what *they* needed to feel fulfilled in their marriages.

My second goal in writing this book is to provide a catalyst **for female breadwinners to gingerly approach their husbands** about uncomfortable topics. My hope is that it will serve as an effective tool for breaking the ice. The concepts laid out in this book may inspire couples to finally begin an honest dialogue. This dialogue should include how this arrangement **makes each of them** *feel.* **Each partner deserves the oppor**tunity to express what he or she needs to feel fulfilled in the marriage. Considering the increasing prevalence of female breadwinners in American relationships, conversations like these may positively alter gender relations as we know it over the next century. Solutions addressing the conundrum of the male ego must come directly from men. Therefore, my journey continues after this book. I will be visiting the men's tent, investigating the male ego, and discovering why it may **be hampering the marriages of female breadwinners across** the world. Honest testimony will shape our journey toward **truth, and will move us one step closer to a place of under**standing and acceptance.

Chapter Six
Sending Out an S.O.S.

THE UNCUSTOMARY CIRCUMSTANCE OF HAVING a female breadwinner as a wife may leave some husbands feeling disoriented and unsure of how to provide for their wives. If this unique category of woman doesn't need financial security, then what *does* she need from her mate? The answer was quite obvious after hearing the candid testimonies of the female breadwinners featured in this book. When asked what they needed most from their mates that they are not currently getting, the response was almost unanimous—*they need support.*

Support is such an ambiguous term that can mean different things to different people, and can have totally different connotations depending on the scenario and the context. What do female breadwinners mean when they say they need support? There will be some variation in the definition of this term depending on the individual woman, her personality, and the marital circumstances. But one common desire prevailed within the group—these women want to feel appreciated for all that they do for their families. To these women, it can feel like the weight of the world is on their shoulders—between career demands, financial responsibilities, and family duties. They want a cheerleader, someone who is proud of their accomplishments and who recognizes their achievements. She needs her husband's actions to confirm that she is indeed supported and understood.

Unfortunately, some female breadwinners experience a reality that is very different from the feelings of support that they desire. Sadly, some can feel as if they are drowning in an undercurrent of jealousy and insecurity that plagues some of these marriages. Some husbands harbor feelings of disdain regarding his wife's accomplishments and success. In her interview, Monica mentioned that she has had to hide her career accomplishments from her husband because he can't "handle" her success. "When I recently told my husband I got a big promotion, [he] just said, 'Oh, ok.' I got no praise or recognition from him, so I called my father thinking [at least] *he* would be proud of me. He said, 'You have to choose between family and career, because a man can only take so much.' "

Monica is torn because she loves her job and feels fulfilled in doing it. She knows that she is smart and worthy of praise **but even her own father scolded her when she achieved tenure** at her academic institution. Such an accolade is *usually* met with celebration and fanfare. But Monica is made to feel that career achievement is like a Scarlett Letter, something to be ashamed of in the eyes of her husband and father. Her husband can't be proud of her because he is insecure. **What is the right answer for women in this circumstance?**

Donna had to face a similar battle in her marriage. **Support was nowhere to be found in the repertoire of treatment** that she regularly received from her husband. Her success was consistently met with jealousy, disdain, and even physical aggression. Donna tried her best to bend in response to her husband's displeasure with her higher income, but she could never seem to placate him sufficiently. "Twice I turned down a salary increase. [My company got bought out by another] and they gave us a raise and everybody was happy—

except me. I took that raise home and I got horrible glares and stares. I received no praise—nothing!! I would go back into the office and say, 'Thank you very much, but it's not a good time for me to get a raise.' I tried to keep things low-key. My family meant everything to me." In Donna's world, her **higher salary and career triumphs were like crosses she had** to bear as she tried to assuage her husband's insecurities.

This concept of female breadwinners being made to feel guilty for their accomplishments can be a perpetual challenge for some wives. It brings to light a glaring double stand**ard that exists in our society with regards to how some mar**ried women can be made to feel about their achievements. A wife's success may be looked upon as "overly "ambitious or emasculating to a certain type of man. Why? If a wife is **intellectually able to achieve a higher standard, then** why shouldn't she? It's simply illogical to think that a woman's intellect has to be bound and tethered just because she is married to a man. Tradition may say that the husband is to be the **more educated, more intellectual, and more omnipotent of** the two—but such traditions are crumbling right before our eyes. There is nothing that you or I can do to stop that!

It is humbling to imagine what a nation like ours could **achieve if it** *fully* recognized and harnessed the intellect of its women. Instead, we live in a society in which women are paid a fraction of men's salaries for the same work and are still made to feel ashamed when they out-earn their husbands. **Wives who have achieved greater success than their hus**bands are still viewed by many as backwards or unacceptable within the framework of a marriage. If a woman can dream it, she should be allowed to achieve it, and still be celebrated by her man and by society at large. Men shouldn't feel *less* *than* just because their wives are successful. If a husband is not satisfied with his own station in life, then he should do something to change instead of trying to sabotage his wife's achievement to boost his own worth.

Luckily, husbands who made their wives feel guilty for their accomplishments represented the minority of circumstances in this book. There are many female breadwinners **whose husbands** *are* genuinely proud of their achievements. But this sense of pride doesn't always translate into her feeling supported. Some husbands still fail to connect with their wives in this area. When asked about her experiences, Teresa replied, "I need support and appreciation. I want to be supported in my endeavors. [I would] like to be accepted for who I am. I don't need finances—I can buy what I want."

But statements like Teresa's can feel vague and confusing to many men—leaving them unable to put their fingers on exactly what she needs. If a female breadwinner is not able to articulate exactly how she needs to be supported, husbands may feel like they are trying to read minds. Under such circumstances, his attempts will undoubtedly fall short of her expectations. So what *does* **this new breed of wife need to feel supported? What will she respond to? If she is sinking like the Titanic under the weight of being the breadwinner in the marriage, how can he try to save her? By sending out an** S.O.S., of course!

S.O.S. is an internationally recognized maritime distress signal that utilizes Morse code. This signal is sent out by a ship's captain to signify that a vessel is sinking, damaged, or otherwise incapacitated. Let's put a unique spin on the abbreviation S.O.S. and place it within the context of the female breadwinner. For the purposes of this chapter, **S.O.S. will stand for "Signs of Support."** S.O.S. are small gestures that a husband can institute to make his wife feel more supported and loved. The role of a female breadwinner can feel overwhelming to many women for many reasons. Some of these **women *do*** exist in a constant state of distress. **They desperately need the support of their husbands to regain a sense of** happiness and fulfillment in their lives.

Some men reading this book are already educated in ways to support their wives. Other husbands may need a little help and inspiration in connecting with the women they love. Small changes incorporated into a husband's repertoire **can be so powerful that it may completely revive a struggling** marriage, or further enhance a relationship that is already healthy. These small adjustments may add mere minutes to a man's daily routine, but these Signs of Support will have a huge impact on a wife's perception of the support she receives in the household and in the marriage.

There is a popular metaphor in society that a working man's job *ends* **when he reaches home, but that a working** woman's second job *begins* at home. Those that ascribe to this metaphor are implying that a working woman's duties of wife/mother/housekeeper/chef/lover can sometimes be as taxing as a second job. Whether accurate or not, it is a common manner of thinking in today's society. Working women, particularly high-earning women, will feel that their second job is easier with a loving and supportive husband by their side.

One point to note is that different wives need different displays of support. Sadly, the actions that constitute Signs of Support cannot be approached in cookie-cutter fashion. Some women need verbal forms of validation like: "I appreciate you," or "I am proud of what you have accomplished," or

"I am grateful for the sacrifices you make for our family." Others need more domestic S.O.S. like more cooking, more help with the kids, or more contributions to household maintenance. Other wives need to feel spoiled with dinners at nice restaurants, vacations, or material gifts. Husbands: It is up to you to discover your wife's needs and the form of support she craves! If you are willing to make your wife's second job feel less overwhelming, read the following vignette, *A Day in the Life.* **Discover how willing husbands can incorporate Signs of Support into their daily routine to better connect with their mates. A little effort can have a major impact on the level of support that she perceives in the marriage.**

A DAY IN THE LIFE

SHANNON WAKES UP TO A blaring alarm clock, disappointed that her rejuvenation has been interrupted. She is still tired from working late in the office last evening. By the time she made it home last night, Bill and the kids were sprawled out asleep in front of the T.V. Shannon had to carry both her son and daughter up to bed and left hubby to enjoy his slumber on the couch. Shannon rises slowly and takes a drink from her bottle of water that she keeps on the bedside table. Bill awoke about an hour ago and was already downstairs in his office working. Over the next hour, Shannon woke **both kids and helped them get showered and dressed for school; the kids made their beds and then scrambled down** the steps with their dog, Bailey, in tow. Shannon took her own shower, got dressed, fixed her hair and joined the rest of the family downstairs. The kids were on the couch watching morning cartoons and Bill remained in his office. The dog looked up at Shannon with a look that could only mean," Feed me, please."

Shannon proceeded to ask the kids what they wanted for breakfast: yogurt and fruit, grilled cheese, or waffles. She started to prepare each child's request. She then looked at the school lunch menu for the week. "Hmm... do you guys want a meatball sub for lunch today?" Her eight-year-old daughter, Alexis, answered, "Yeah, I like those meatball subs. They taste like pizza." Miles, her ten-year-old son was a picky eater and answered with an emphatic, "No! That stuff is gross!" As the waffles toasted, Shannon began fixing a lunch and snack for Miles and just a snack for Alexis. Shannon poured orange juice for them both and the kids set the table for breakfast. Peanut butter and jelly for Miles was his standard request for lunch. She placed both lunch boxes on the table by the door. Waffles popped up, were buttered quickly and slid onto plates for the kids to devour. Shannon's stomach grumbled a bit, what could she eat that was quick? She'd pick up something later. Bailey, their German Shepherd, was still standing there staring at Shannon as his tail wagged excitedly. Shannon quickly filled Bailey's bowls with food and water. Next task was **book bag check to be sure that all the homework items** were signed and in their correct folders. Bill came out of his office and Shannon asked," Do you want a waffle, hon?" Bill declined stating that waffles weren't on the "workout menu." He grabbed some juice from the fridge and went back in his office. Shannon checked the clock. "Okay kids, time to head out. We don't wanna be late." The kids scraped their plates into the trash can which was nearly full. "Don't forget today is trash day!" Shannon announced loudly to Bill in his office. The kids dumped their dishes into the sink. As Shannon and the kids piled into the garage, Bill gave Shannon and Alexis a kiss and gave Miles a pound. Shannon pulled out of the driveway and gazed down her tree-lined street noticing the green trash cans all in a row at the curbs.

Shannon dropped both kids at school and then headed to work downtown. Since she hadn't had time to eat, she grabbed a coffee in the lobby on her way upstairs to her corner office.

The next eight hours consisted of Shannon leading a team of 20 individuals. Her company was in the middle of a merger, they were acquiring another law firm and Shannon had to be on top of her game. She was the lead for three meetings throughout the day, one of which was an impromptu meeting, and fielded a total of 19 phone calls. She had a small tuna salad for lunch; she needed three cups of coffee throughout the day to stay amped and counteract fatigue. By 5:00 p.m., Shannon was physically dehydrated, emotionally drained, and was starting to run out of steam altogether. She glanced at her watch. "Crap!" She had 30 minutes to make it to the kids' aftercare. She didn't want to pay $20 again for **being late! She shut down her laptop, crammed her papers in** her briefcase and raced to the lobby. Bill called her cell phone as she exited the elevator. "Hey, honey! How was your day?" Shannon and Bill chatted for a moment about their respective workdays. "What's for dinner?" Bill asked. "I want to get my taste buds ready." Shannon had no clue what was for dinner. How could she focus on dinner when all she could think about today was the ramifications of her company's merger? She mumbled, "Mmm... probably chicken of some sort. I will be home by 6:30, okay?" Bill answered, "Okay, drive safely. Love you."

Shannon drove up to aftercare and the kids were at the curb waiting. It was 6:00 p.m. exactly, no cash needed to be paid today for tardiness! Shannon reveled in that satisfaction of being on-time, but just for a second. "How was your day, Miles? Alexis?" The kids gave meager details about their day and exclaimed almost in sync: "I'm hungry! What's for dinner?" Shannon was so tired from her busy day that all she **wanted to do was sit down and put her feet up for the rest** of the night. She envisioned herself placing a big plate of Ramen Noodles on the dining room table and saying, "Bon appetite!" to her family before she retreated to her bedroom! **The car behind her honked and Shannon snapped back to re**ality. She tried to recall what was in the fridge; she hoped she had at least one bag of frozen or "steam in the bag" veggies left. She could accompany that with 90-second, microwaveable, Uncle Ben's rice.

Shannon pulled her SUV into the driveway and noticed one of the porch lights next to the garage had burned out. She would have to remember to change it out on Saturday. Shannon walked into the house through the garage door. The kids passed their father's office with a, "Hi Daddy! We're home!" The kids were always good about starting homework as soon as they got home. Shannon walked toward the kitchen after kicking off her heels. Her back hurt as she bent over to retrieve the frozen chicken from the bottom freezer drawer. She placed the chicken pieces in a bowl and set the timer on her microwave to defrost. She glanced over the kids' shoulders at the day's homework assignments and prepared herself for the myriad of questions that were sure to come. "Mommy, what does 'pollution' mean?" Miles asked with a puzzled look. "It means particles, gases, or other stuff that gets into the air and makes it dirty." That was the best answer Shannon could come up with at that moment. She looked at Alexis practicing her writing and said, "Don't forget to put a small space after every period, Lexi."

Shannon checked on the chicken in the microwave. Her head was starting to throb, probably because she hadn't managed to get that last cup of coffee before she left work. She checked the fridge for the frozen vegetable options. She **had to be sure the family got something green with every** meal. She was pleased to find Miles' favorite: leaf spinach. She would add garlic and a pat of butter, just liked he liked it. Bill came out of his office and kissed Shannon on her neck, saying, "How was your day, sweets?" His hand brushed her **behind and he walked over to the couch and picked up to-**day's paper. He plopped down in his favorite spot on their **leather couch and was quickly accompanied by the dog who** loved to be scratched on the side of his neck.

Shannon chose a myriad of spices to sprinkle on the chicken over which she drizzled olive oil and craftily found a perfect spot for each boneless breast in the grill pan. Miles yelled out "STOP!!" as he slapped Alexis' notebook that she continued to push over to his side of the table. "This is my space! Mommy, Lexi won't stop agitating me!" "Hey, be nice to each other! Lexi, gives Miles his space. You know he hates to feel crowded!" Shannon looked back to find the chicken browning too quickly in the pan. She quickly added the additional olive oil that she needed to quell the scorching. As the kids closed their notebooks, Shannon said, "Hey, don't close it up until I check it for each of you." "Mommy, is our dinner going to be burned up? If so, I wanna have pizza again!" Alexis laughed. Bill looked over to her and said, "Geez, Shannon, can you turn on the fan? It smells terrible!" Shannon knew that the chicken could be salvaged if she placed the pan on a cool burner for a second.

The kids' homework met her approval so she signed the necessary papers and returned the folders to each book bag. Shannon sliced open the bag of veggies and placed the spinach in a pan to be sautéed. She popped the 90-second whole grain rice in the microwave and pushed START. She said to the kids: "Set the table. The food is almost ready." "Aww... Mom! This is my favorite episode of Sponge Bob! Do I have to?" "Yes, you do! Unless, you don't wanna eat!" Shannon snapped. The dog came and stood in her path and looked up as if to say, "Feed me, please." She brushed the dog out of the way as she sliced up the grilled chicken breasts. She artfully plated chicken breast slices over a bed of spinach topped with dried parsley and spooned some rice on the side of each plate. Bill put down his newspaper and came into the kitchen, grabbed the drinking glasses from the cupboard, and filled each with iced green tea. The kids were already seated at the dinner table. Shannon quickly scooped up a cup of dog food and emptied it in the dog's bowl. She and Bill joined the kids at the table. "Say your grace, kids." Each of them bowed their heads in unison, recited the prayer, and then dug into the food. Despite the brief scorching, the chicken was moist and flavorful. "Tastes good, babe," Bill mumbled with food in his mouth. "Yeah, Mommy. Especially the spinach!" Miles exclaimed.

After dinner, Bill and the kids cleared the table and placed the dishes in the sink. Shannon wiped down the stove and cleaned up her cooking space. She noticed the kitchen trashcan was overflowing. "Guess we missed trash day today,"

Shannon said to Bill. He didn't comment and walked back in his office just in time for an evening conference call with one of his business partners. Shannon removed the trash bag from the can and placed it in the garage. Shannon peeked her head into Bill's office. "Can you clear the sink after your conference call?" Shannon asked Bill in a whisper. He nodded affirmatively as he continued his call.

"Okay, time for baths! Who's going first into the Jacuzzi tub?" "I am this time!" hollered Alexis. "Miles got to do it last time!" The kids stumbled clumsily up the steps and collected their bedclothes. Within 40 minutes, each child was washed, teeth brushed, and was in bed ready for a story. The three of them, Shannon, Miles, and Alexis, piled in Miles's bed. "Mommy, can you read Junie B. Jones this time? Miles got to pick a boy book last time." Miles nodded and said, "Okay, that's fine with me. I like Junie B., even if she is a girl," as he wrinkled his nose. Shannon smiled; she loved when her kids could agree on something. The dog came in the room and plopped himself on the floor between the kids' beds. After two exciting tales of Junie B. adventures, Alexis was asleep, Miles was weary-eyed, and even Shannon's eyelids felt heavy. Shannon rose slowly and placed little Alexis in her own bed. She turned to Miles. "Say your prayers before you fall asleep. I love you. Sweet dreams."

Shannon turned out the light and pulled the door almost closed. She exhaled as she retreated to her own bedroom and turned on the ceiling fan. She turned on the shower and found her most comfortable nightgown. She took a relaxing shower, lathered on some Tahitian vanilla lotion, washed the make-up from her face, and found her fuzzy slippers. All she **could think about was turning out the lights, climbing into**

bed, and watching HGTV or CNN to help her mind relax before falling asleep. She forgot she had left her purse and her iPhone downstairs after dinner. Shannon walked down the mahogany stairs that were dustier than she cared to realize. She noticed Bill asleep on the couch in front of the television with his head bobbing and dishes still in the sink. She decided **she would have to deal with those dishes tomorrow—she** was simply too tired tonight. Shannon crept carefully back up the steps. She avoided the fifth step that has been in disrepair for some time and creaks loudly, being careful not to wake Bill. Shannon pulled back the covers on her California king bed, climbed onto her Egyptian cotton sheets, and was **in a dream state within minutes—far from corporate take**overs and scorched chicken.

A DAY IN THE LIFE: TAKE TWO

SHANNON WAKES UP TO A blaring alarm clock, disappointed that her rejuvenation has been interrupted. She is still tired from working late in the office last evening. By the time she made it home last night, Bill and the kids were sprawled out asleep in front of the T.V. Shannon had to carry both her son and daughter up to bed and left hubby to enjoy his slumber on the couch.

(S.O.S. #1: Why were the kids not in bed when she got home late from the office? Children function best when they follow a nightly bedtime routine. Even in Shannon's absence, this routine should continue to ensure that the kids are getting sufficient sleep. Following the "bedtime routine" is a display of responsible behavior that comes along with successful par-

enting. Bill can show support for the sacrifices that Shannon makes for the family by ensuring that small family tasks will be handled dependably in her absence.)

Shannon rises slowly and takes a drink from her bottle of water that she keeps on the bedside table. Bill awoke about an hour ago and was already downstairs in his office working. Over the next hour, Shannon woke both kids and helped **them get showered and dressed for school; the kids made their beds and then scrambled down the steps with their dog**, Bailey, in tow. Shannon took her own shower, got dressed, fixed her hair and joined the rest of the family downstairs. **The kids were on the couch watching morning cartoons and** Bill remained in his office. The dog looked up at Shannon with a look that could only mean," Feed me, please."

***(S.O.S. #2:** Shannon may interpret Bill's absence from the kids' morning routine as selfish and inconsiderate. Why should he have the unilateral luxury to retreat into his office instead of assisting Shannon with preparing the kids for school? There's no fairness in this scenario. The household should function as a unit, particularly when they both have demanding work schedules. An appropriate S.O.S. would be for Bill to wake up early and work in his office until time for the kids to wake. He has an opportunity to show great support to his wife by coming upstairs to help his children get ready for school alongside his wife. It is an unspoken way to say, "Yes, I have work commitments, but supporting you and my family is a priority.")*

Shannon proceeded to ask the kids what they wanted for breakfast: yogurt and fruit, grilled cheese, or waffles. She started to prepare each child's request. She then looked at the school lunch menu for the week. "Hmm... do you guys want a meatball sub for lunch today?" Her eight-year-old daughter, Alexis, answered, "Yeah, I like those meatball subs. They taste like pizza." Miles, her ten-year-old son was a picky eater and answered with an emphatic, "No! That stuff is gross!" As the waffles toasted, Shannon began fixing a lunch and snack for Miles and just a snack for Alexis. Shannon poured orange juice for them both and the kids set the table for breakfast. Peanut butter and jelly for Miles was his standard request for lunch. She placed both lunch boxes on the table by the door. Waffles popped up, were buttered quickly and slid onto plates for the kids to devour.

(S.O.S. #3: *Bill should come out of the office and be active in preparing the children's breakfast and stocking lunch boxes. A team effort helps Shannon feel supported and appreciated. Even small gestures like packing cookies for the kids' lunch or buttering the waffles or pouring the juice speaks volumes in the female breadwinner's love language.)*

Shannon's stomach grumbled a bit, what could she eat that was quick? She'd pick up something later. Bailey, their German Shepherd, was still standing there staring at Shannon as his tail wagged excitedly. Shannon quickly filled Bailey's bowls with food and water. Next task was book bag **check to be sure that all the homework items were signed** and in their correct folders. Bill came out of his office and Shannon asked," Do you want a waffle, hon?" Bill declined stating that waffles weren't on the "workout menu." He grabbed some juice from the fridge and went back in his office. Shannon checked the clock. "Okay kids, time to head out. We don't wanna be late." The kids scraped their plates into the trash can which was nearly full. "Don't forget today is trash day!" Shannon announced loudly to Bill in his office. The kids dumped their dishes into the sink. As Shannon and the kids piled into the garage, Bill gave Shannon and Alexis a kiss and gave Miles a pound. Shannon pulled out of the driveway and gazed down her tree-lined street noticing the green trash cans all in a row at the curbs.

*(**S.O.S. #4:** If Bill can be consistent by having his trashcan at the curb on time, Shannon will feel that cleanliness of his castle is important to her husband as the King. This is a characteristic of an effective leader. While the duty of trash collection is a chore traditionally relegated to the male gender, it still racks up big points for some women as a show of support.)*

Shannon dropped both kids at school and then headed to work downtown. Since she hadn't had time to eat, she grabbed a coffee in the lobby on her way upstairs to her corner office.

*(**S.O.S. #5:** Due to the morning's time constraints, Shannon has only had time for a cup of coffee for her own breakfast. Over time, she may start to feel resentful of Bill's preoccupation with "self" in the mornings. If she had more assistance in the morning, Shannon could have prepared a more suitable meal for herself and her husband.)*

The next eight hours consisted of Shannon leading a team of 20 individuals. Her company was in the middle of a merger, they were acquiring another law firm and Shannon had to be on top of her game. She was the lead for three meetings throughout the day, one of which was an impromptu meeting, and fielded a total of 19 phone calls. She had a small tuna salad for lunch; she needed three cups of coffee throughout the day to stay amped and counteract fatigue. By 5:00 p.m., Shannon was physically dehydrated, emotionally drained, and was starting to run out of steam altogether. She glanced at her watch. "Crap!" She had 30 minutes to make it to the kids' aftercare. She didn't want to pay $20 again for **being late! She shut down her laptop, crammed her papers in** her briefcase and raced to the lobby. Bill called her cell phone as she exited the elevator. "Hey, honey! How was your day?" Shannon and Bill chatted for a moment about their respective workdays. "What's for dinner?" Bill asked. "I want to get my taste buds ready." Shannon had no clue what was for dinner. How could she focus on dinner when all she could think about today was the ramifications of her company's merger? She mumbled, "Mmm... probably chicken of some sort. I will be home by 6:30, okay?" Bill answered, "Okay, drive safely. Love you."

*(**S.O.S. #6:** Bill is just as capable of fixing dinner as Shannon, especially if she already has the added task of picking the kids up from school. There should be a voluntary division of household labor when both husband and wife are working outside of the home. Shannon's law firm is in the middle of a merger; she is stressed and pre-occupied with business. She needs a mate who can sense her frustrations and will take extra steps to support her during this tumultuous period. If Bill loves his wife, then her psychological and emotional well-being should*

be of key importance to him. Small gestures on his part can help his wife feel supported and appreciated for all the hard work she puts into running the household as well as her career.)

Shannon drove up to aftercare and the kids were at the curb waiting. It was 6:00 p.m. exactly... no cash needed to be paid today for tardiness! Shannon reveled in that satisfaction of being on-time, but just for a second.

(S.O.S. #7: *Can Bill arrange his workday to pick the kids up from school, especially on days when Shannon's workday runs late? As a parent, Bill has equal responsibility for addressing the children's needs. He should not view carpooling the kids as a "wifely" duty. He should seriously consider whether he is in a position to take over that duty daily or at least a few times a week.)*

"How was your day, Miles? Alexis?" The kids gave meager details about their day and exclaimed almost in sync: "I'm hungry! What's for dinner?" Shannon was so tired from her **busy day that all she wanted to do was sit down and put her** feet up for the rest of the night. She envisioned herself placing a big plate of Ramen Noodles on the dining room table and saying, "Bon appetite!" to her family before she retreat**ed to her bedroom! The car behind her honked and Shan**non snapped back to reality. She tried to recall what was in the fridge; she hoped she had at least one bag of frozen or "steam in the bag" veggies left. She could accompany that with 90-second, microwaveable, Uncle Ben's rice.

Shannon pulled her SUV into the driveway and noticed one of the porch lights next to the garage had burned out. She would have to remember to change it out on Saturday.

(S.O.S. #8: Why hasn't Bill noticed that the porch light is out? If Bill can change that garage light and maintain a household that is in good repair, Shannon will have more confidence in her leader. It is important for a breadwinner to feel that her husband as the head of household can handle small tasks to improve household maintenance.)

Shannon walked into the house through the garage door. The kids passed their father's office with a, "Hi Daddy! We're home!" The kids were always good about starting homework as soon as they got home. Shannon walked toward the kitchen after kicking off her heels. Her back hurt as she bent over to retrieve the frozen chicken from the bottom freezer drawer. She placed the chicken pieces in a bowl and set the timer on her microwave to defrost.

(S.O.S. #9: If Bill is already home, he should take the initiative to start dinner planning in some fashion. Even if he can't cook, he can at least thaw out the meat and have a packet of seasoning or a jar of marinade on the counter. This would show that he is engaged to some degree in the dinner preparation process.)

She glanced over the kids' shoulders at the day's homework assignments and prepared herself for the myriad of questions that were sure to come. "Mommy, what does 'pollution' mean?" Miles asked with a puzzled look. "It means particles, gases, or other stuff that gets into the air and makes it dirty." That was the best answer Shannon could come up with at that moment. She looked at Alexis practicing her writing and said, "Don't forget to put a small space after every period, Lexi."

Shannon checked on the chicken in the microwave. Her head was starting to throb, probably because she hadn't managed to get that last cup of coffee before she left work. She checked the fridge for the frozen vegetable options. She **had to be sure the family got something green with every** meal. She was pleased to find Miles' favorite: leaf spinach. She would add garlic and a pat of butter, just liked he liked it. Bill came out of his office and kissed Shannon on her neck, saying, "How was your day, sweets?" His hand brushed her **behind and he walked over to the couch and picked up to-**day's paper. He plopped down in his favorite spot on their **leather couch and was quickly accompanied by the dog who** loved to be scratched on the side of his neck.

(S.O.S. #10: Um, excuse me? If Shannon and Bill have both had a long day at work, it feels very unfair for Bill to plop down on the sofa. Shannon's feet are SCREAMING because she's been on them all day and her back is killing her; she is also exhausted. They should BOTH participate in dinner preparation and assisting the kids with their homework.)

Shannon chose a myriad of spices to sprinkle on the chicken over which she drizzled olive oil and craftily found a perfect spot for each boneless breast in the grill pan. Miles yelled out "STOP!!" as he slapped Alexis' notebook that she continued to push over to his side of the table. "This is my space! Mommy, Lexi won't stop agitating me!" "Hey, be nice to each other! Lexi, gives Miles his space. You know he hates to feel crowded!"

(S.O.S. #11: *Shannon is using coffee as a source of energy because she is exhausted. Bill should be more observant of his wife's overwhelming schedule including demanding office duties, child-rearing, and domestic duties. If things are left unchecked, Shannon may shut down both emotionally and physically. She needs a break; Bill would be able to recognize that if he tried harder to stay tuned in.)*

Shannon looked back to find the chicken browning too quickly in the pan. She quickly added the additional olive oil that she needed to quell the scorching. As the kids closed their notebooks, Shannon said, "Hey, don't close it up until I check it for each of you." "Mommy, is our dinner going to be burned up? If so, I wanna have pizza again!" Alexis laughed. Bill looked over to her and said, "Geez, Shannon, can you turn on the fan? It smells terrible!" Shannon knew that the **chicken could be salvaged if she placed the pan on a cool burner** for a second.

(S.O.S. #12: *Bill should refrain from complaining about the chicken burning or anything else for that matter, particularly since he is doing nothing to contribute to dinner or with the kids' well-being at the moment. Complaints make Shannon feel as though all her hard work and sacrifice is not appreciated by the kids—"If you burn the chicken, can we have pizza?"—or by her husband, Bill.)*

The kids' homework met her approval so she signed the necessary papers and returned the folders to each book bag. **Shannon sliced open the bag of veggies and placed the spinach in a pan to be sautéed.** She popped the 90-second whole grain rice in the microwave and pushed START. She said to the kids: "Set the table. The food is almost ready." "Aww... Mom! This is my favorite episode of Sponge Bob! Do I have to?" "Yes, you do! Unless, you don't wanna eat!" Shannon snapped. The dog came and stood in her path and looked up as if to say, "Feed me, please." She brushed the dog out of the way as she sliced up the grilled chicken breasts.

(S.O.S. #13: A dog is man's best friend. Why can't Bill see that the dog is hungry and feed him?)

She artfully plated chicken breast slices over a bed of **spinach topped with dried parsley and spooned some rice** on the side of each plate. Bill put down his newspaper and **came into the kitchen, grabbed the drinking glasses from the** cupboard, and filled each with iced green tea. The kids were already seated at the dinner table. Shannon quickly scooped up a cup of dog food and emptied it in the dog's bowl. She and Bill joined the kids at the table. "Say your grace, kids." **Each of them bowed their heads in unison, recited the prayer,** and then dug into the food. Despite the brief scorching, the chicken was moist and flavorful. "Tastes good, babe," Bill mumbled with food in his mouth. "Yeah, Mommy. Especially the spinach!" Miles exclaimed.

After dinner, Bill and the kids cleared the table and placed the dishes in the sink. Shannon wiped down the stove and cleaned up her cooking space. She noticed the kitchen trashcan was overflowing. "Guess we missed trash day today," Shannon said to Bill. He didn't comment and walked back in his office just in time for an evening conference call with one of his business partners.

(S.O.S. #14: Taking out the trash is probably the most masculine job in the entire household! When Shannon sees that this chore is consistently not done, she interprets that as weakness in her mate. This is a trait of a poor leader and she feels resentful.)

Shannon removed the trash bag from the can and placed it in the garage. Shannon peeked her head into Bill's office. "Can you clear the sink after your conference call?" Shannon asked Bill in a whisper. He nodded affirmatively as he continued his call.

"Okay, time for baths! Who's going first into the Jacuzzi tub?" "I am this time!" hollered Alexis. "Miles got to do it last time!" The kids stumbled clumsily up the steps and collected their bedclothes. Within 40 minutes, each child was washed, teeth brushed, and was in bed ready for a story. The three of them, Shannon, Miles, and Alexis, piled in Miles's bed. "Mommy, can you read Junie B. Jones this time? Miles got to pick a boy book last time." Miles nodded and said, "Okay, that's fine with me. I like Junie B., even if she is a girl," as he wrinkled his nose. Shannon smiled; she loved when her kids could agree on something. The dog came in the room and plopped himself on the floor between the kids' beds. After two exciting tales of Junie B. adventures, Alexis was asleep,

Miles was weary-eyed, and even Shannon's eyelids felt heavy. Shannon rose slowly and placed little Alexis in her own bed. She turned to Miles. "Say your prayers before you fall asleep. I love you. Sweet dreams."

Shannon turned out the light and pulled the door almost closed. She exhaled as she retreated to her own bedroom and turned on the ceiling fan. She turned on the shower and found her most comfortable nightgown. She took a relaxing shower, lathered on some Tahitian vanilla lotion, washed the make-up from her face, and found her fuzzy slippers. All she **could think about was turning out the lights, climbing into** bed, and watching HGTV or CNN to help her mind relax before falling asleep. She forgot she had left her purse and her iPhone downstairs after dinner. Shannon walked down the mahogany stairs that were dustier than she cared to realize. She noticed Bill asleep on the couch in front of the television with his head bobbing and dishes still in the sink. She decid**ed she would have to deal with those dishes tomorrow—she** was simply too tired tonight.

(S.O.S. #15: Bill agreed to clear the sink after dinner. So why is he falling asleep on the couch with this chore left undone? Shannon cooked the meal and fairness dictates that Bill should clean up the kitchen afterwards.)

Shannon crept carefully back up the steps. She avoided the fifth step that has been in disrepair for some time and creaks loudly, being careful not to wake Bill. Shannon pulled **back the covers on her California king bed, climbed onto her** Egyptian cotton sheets, and was in a dream state within minutes—far from corporate take-overs and scorched chicken.

(**S.O.S. #16:** *Bill should have taken care of this rickety step some time ago. If you want to claim the title of the head of household, it takes sacrifice and timely troubleshooting skills. It is not a right, it is a privilege, and it should be taken seriously.*)

WHAT LIES BENEATH

THERE ARE MANY FEMALE BREADWINNERS who share the same psychological space as Shannon: feeling unfulfilled and unappreciated. She needs the support of her husband and her family to cope effectively with life's stressors, particularly when combining the traditional wifely duties with those of the household breadwinner. Throughout this hypothetical vignette, there were many missed opportunities for Bill to connect with his wife and to confirm his love and support. If Bill is willing to commit to improving his marriage, adopting these simple Signs of Support (S.O.S.) can elevate Shannon and Bill's marriage to a higher and more fulfilling place. Bill **may not even be aware that his wife is longing for greater** happiness and support. But as the head of household and the **protector for the family, he should consider his awareness of** his wife's happiness as a priority.

Signs of Support can prevent female breadwinners from feeling like the pack mule of the family. Without adequate **displays of support from their mates, they can begin to feel** as if they are getting "dumped on" by their husbands, left to pick up whatever pieces he fails to put together. Instead, the **female breadwinner wants to feel as if she is part of a team—** with a dependable teammate who is willing to sacrifice for her and the family. Female breadwinners can sometimes feel as if the weight of the world is on their shoulders. This **unique category of woman wants her accomplishments, her** hard work, and sacrifice for the family to be acknowledged and praised. Simple phrases like, "I appreciate what you do for our family," "I am proud of your accomplishments," "Can I support you in any way," and "I realize that you work hard for this family," can have a huge impact on a female breadwinner's self-esteem and pride.

In certain circumstances, the breadwinning wife can be made to feel guilty for out-earning her mate, as if she is making life hard for him by emasculating him in eyes of the world. She may need validation from time to time that she is doing a good thing. By exhibiting Signs of Support, her mate has the **power to make her feel supported in a cold world,** thus giving her the permission she needs to feel proud.

When a captain's ship is sinking, he frantically sends out an S.O.S., a universal distress signal to notify appropriate authorities that his vessel is in immediate need of support. In the face of career demands, family responsibilities, financial pressures, and domestic duties, female breadwinners can also experience a feeling similar to that of drowning. The **female breadwinners interviewed for this book expressed a** unanimous desire for more support in their marriages. When **asked what was lacking in their marriages, support and appre**ciation were prioritized for every woman. Regretfully, many **female breadwinners fail to successfully impart their desire** for more support to their mates. The preceding vignette, A **Day in the Life, may have provided a greater sense of awareness about the Signs of Support that women like Shannon** need to feel fulfilled in a marriage. The S.O.S. that the female breadwinner desires is rooted in actions, not words, and can be effectively mastered with minimal effort if her partner is willing. A man who dedicates himself to adopting the principle **Signs of Support as described in this chapter** will likely realize a healthier connection with his wife today, resulting in the creation of a greater marital bond moving toward the future.

Chapter Seven
When Life Hands You Lemons

LET'S INVESTIGATE HOW MARRIAGES OR relationships containing a female breadwinner differ from a traditional arrangement. The answer is varied and complex depending on the individuals involved. But there are some common challenges and resolutions that resonate across the board. For instance, each partner's expectations of gender roles in the marriage must be more flexible than a traditional couple. For many of us, gender-related expectations of marital roles were developed and solidified during our formative years. Some of these expectations can be preserved in marriages containing a female breadwinner; other expectations will have to be modified; and still others must be shed altogether.

Historically, the term "provider" was used to define a man's role or position in the marriage, conceptually placing him in a box. He was the "provider" of the income, the financial security, and subsequently the leadership for the household. In my opinion, this term has become outdated in a modern society. Due to changes in the American economy over the past several decades, the "two-income" household is now defined as the national standard. In most modern **families, both male** *and* **female partners contribute to the financial solvency of the household, and have been doing so** for some time. Therefore, the term "co-provider" is a more **accurate descriptor, even when the male boasts the higher** income.

So, when the income hierarchy in the marriage shifts in favor of the woman, how do the mates of female breadwinners define themselves? This becomes a difficult question and can be a struggle for any man to answer. In my opinion, these men must shed the obsolete title of "provider," a term that is beginning to feel more antiquated with each passing day. A man's worth in a marriage or relationship supersedes dollars and cents. Men must rediscover the splendor of what it means to be a man—his strength, his fearlessness, his confidence. They must recognize the myriad of ways that they enhance their mate's existence. In a nutshell, they must redefine themselves and reinvent themselves within the context of a new reality!

How can female breadwinners encourage their mates to view their circumstance as something other than a detriment? It starts by encouraging them to change their perception of their circumstances. Do these men interpret the circumstance of being married to a female breadwinner as a glass half-empty or half-full? The mates of breadwinners have a unique opportunity to carve out a new identity for themselves. They are able to step outside the box and create an existence beyond the label of "provider" in a traditional sense. If approached correctly, his new identity has the potential to catapult him towards greater happiness and fulfillment in life. How many of us get locked into a place of employment in order to keep the bills paid, without experiencing true fulfillment in life? Such a lackluster existence probably describes most of our nation's population. The mates of female breadwinners have more flexibility than most men regarding how they may choose to make a living.

A variety of circumstances could have relieved these husbands of the shackles of breadwinner status. And whether he appreciates it or not, because of his wife's financial capabilities, he may have less of a load to carry as it relates to household finances. In essence, he has been given more freedom in life compared with most husbands. He is no longer boxed into the position of "provider." As a result of this freedom, these men are able to slow down long enough to dream. If **men can see their circumstance of having a higher-earning** wife as empowering, they can maximize the benefits of their circumstance and seek to improve their own station in life.

If a man likes to cook, he may have the financial flexibility to cut back on work hours and seek culinary instruction to further that craft. By making a choice to embrace his passion, he reinvents himself. This can lead to greater fulfillment and overall happiness in his life and in the marriage. And may also lead to unique employment opportunities in the future. Melissa's position as the breadwinner in her marriage allows **her husband the freedom to pursue a career path outside of** his academic degree, but one that brings him great joy and contentment. Melissa's husband was able to move beyond **the feelings of regret that plague some men who have had to** relinquish breadwinner status in their marriages. He recognizes that true fulfillment in life does not come from money, but instead comes from following one's passion in life. He should be applauded for appreciating his situation for what it truly is—an opportunity for greater fulfillment, despite outdated societal labels regarding marital roles.

If a husband has an entrepreneurial spirit, he may have enough financial support from his wife to consider starting a small business in a field in which he is passionate. This was the case in my own marriage. When my husband was laid off toward the end of the recession, I was able to carry household finances for a few years. This allowed my husband greater freedom to thoughtfully craft his next steps after the lay-off. He did not have to scramble and rush to find a job that may not have been a good fit for him or for the family. After much discussion and quite a bit of prayer, I encouraged **him to combine his passions for golf and travel, and channel** them into the creation of a small business. He had the cour- **age to reinvent himself within the context of a new reality** by becoming an entrepreneur. He is now a successful luxury golf tour operator, enjoying life to a much greater degree than he ever could have imagined working for someone else. In addition to living out a dream by doing what he loves, he has created a new source of revenue for the household. This will **generate greater wealth for our family as we move into the** future.

Female breadwinners have been the saving grace for so many families as the nation recovers from its most recent economic recession. Thanks to the earning potential of this newest category of wife, many husbands who were jobless during the country's economic drought were fortunate in being able to maintain financial footing. Cicely's husband was also laid off during the recession. But for personal reasons, he chose not to seek reentry to his former career path. That couple made a joint decision that if Cicely's husband was happiest in a non-traditional career, then she was willing to try to make it work. This breadwinner understands how her husband thinks and what makes him tick. She recognized that a traditional career path failed to bring her husband the happiness that she desired for him.

At some point in their marriages, many wives have witnessed their husbands withstand a dead-end job in order to keep food on the table. I know I have. Thankless, unrewarding occupations can create a husband who is overly stressed, **depressed, angry, exhausted, and in compromised health** physically, psychologically, and emotionally. Cicely and her husband made the pragmatic decision to prioritize happiness in their marriage. "He has said, 'Do you want me to get a job?' and I know that is going to make him unhappy so the relationship is not going to be better [if he does]. I really want him to be happy." Cicely recognizes that if she keeps the man she loves happy, she will enjoy a more rewarding relationship and a more fulfilling home life.

If the husband of a female breadwinner has had dreams of pursuing higher education, he may have a mate with whom he can share the financial burdens of life while he furthers his learning. With his wife's support, he can pursue a degree that will undoubtedly open up opportunities for greater wealth and fulfillment. Without the financial burdens of being the "provider," these men have more opportunities than their counterparts in a traditional relationship. Husbands of female breadwinners can enjoy the unique circumstance of having a mate who can provide both emotional *and* financial support needed to reach their own dreams.

Our opinions about our own state of existence in life are guided by perception. Female breadwinners can help their **mates view their circumstance as something gained, not** something lost. Whether they recognize it or not, the mates **of breadwinning wives have gained greater opportunity and** promise in their own lives. If they have the bravery to maximize their circumstances, these men can make their new reality work for them and for the marriage.

Chapter Eight
Dr. Jekyll & Mrs. Hyde

THE TITLE OF THIS CHAPTER refers to a famous 1930s film and is meant to describe a unique phenomenon that some female breadwinners may encounter when transitioning from the workplace back to their home environment. The film portrays a man who repeatedly transforms from a mild-mannered individual to a homicidal maniac after drinking a magic potion. Although I am not intentionally comparing the behavior of a female breadwinner with that of a maniac, I am using the comparison to address a very real and very valid internal struggle that female breadwinners may experience every now and then.

To explain this concept, I will use a scenario experienced by a couple that I know very well: Natalie and Mark. Natalie is a surgeon and is the breadwinner in her marriage. Her husband, Mark, is an entrepreneur. The couple was visiting Mark's mother out of town and an unexpected flood was discovered in her guest bathroom. Cosmetic damage was imminent and both husband and wife sprang into action to help with the emergency. Out of nowhere, the Mark turns to Natalie and says, "Go sit down!" as he proceeds to handle to emergency on his own without her help.

Although the wife said nothing at the time, she was immensely insulted and hurt. While Mark may have simply been trying to "handle" the situation like a man, Natalie interpreted his actions as a form of dismissal. She felt dejected, as if she was being treated like a child. This female breadwinner encounters emergencies everyday, **literally holding the life of patients in her hands**. Despite the fact that she is adept at handling life or death situations as a part of her career, she felt that her talents and expertise were being marginalized by her husband simply because she is a woman.

Men reading this story may not relate to why this situation touches on what can feel like an internal struggle for Natalie. Have you ever considered that fact that the female **breadwinner in a marriage may be living a double life? Think** about it for a second. As a surgeon each day from 9:00 a.m. to 5:00 p.m., Natalie must assume the characteristics of a leader, and must do so convincingly. She has to "walk like a man and talk like a man" to be accepted by her male peers in the surgical suite. At times she has had to fight like a junkyard dog to advance in her career. She must refrain from showing vulnerability or weakness in the cut-throat career environment. **So, how easy do you think it is for her to come home and transform into a submissive Stepford wife once she crosses the threshold of her home? Not easy at all!**

Any undercover agent will tell you that existing between **two worlds can be extremely challenging! But female bread**winners are expected to do it every day and sometimes with very little support from their mates. Her husband may look at her and think, "Why are you so mean?" or "What's with the attitude?" or "You act like you wanna wear the pants in this family!" Well, what he may be witnessing is his female breadwinner's subconscious inability to shed the impervious armor that she needs to survive in the workplace. She may be experiencing some difficulty returning to her natural state of femininity when she rejoins her husband and kids at home.

What expectations do husbands have of these breadwinners? **Do they expect a female CEO of a Fortune 500 company** to automatically cast aside the power and influence that she exudes at the office just as she puts the key in the door at home? There are no right or wrong answers here, only an honest admission of one's expectations. Does a man expect **a renowned female police chief who holds the fates of dangerous criminals in her hands on a daily basis, to come home and bake him a pie because he had a bad day at the factory?** If your answer is yes, then be honest. But just know that you **have your work cut out for you! It can be done but you must** assist in getting your woman back to her happy place when she is in your presence. It can certainly be accomplished if there is mutual respect and love between you. But it has to be done the right way.

If a female breadwinner arrives home in a "manly" sort of mood, how does a husband get this point across? A female breadwinner who may be a leader in her career, possesses advanced degrees, and has high intelligence, will rebel against being told, "Stop acting like a man." But as her husband, ONLY YOU can help her work through this dilemma—a dilemma that she may not even realize exists within her. Her man has the power to help her feel soft again, to help her **regain her femininity, to help her rediscover her vulnerability,** to help her reclaim her womanhood.

Try lightening the mood by creating a humorous buzz phrase that you both learn to associate with this Mrs. Hyde behavior. If you say something like, "Your Midol is showing," you both can laugh it off and regroup. Once she hears you utter those buzz words, she will understand that her mood is too forceful for the safe zone of your home environment. She should be able to keep that bravado in the workplace.

If you can help your female breadwinner to snap back into a more feminine reality, she may be more loving, more supportive, more domesticated, and more sensual. The two of you may develop more balance in your marriage if you currently feel that there is a power struggle in the household. But even more effective than words in this scenario are a husband's actions. Here is some advice on how you can get started:

Blooms. Surprise her with flowers. Research her favorite flowers in advance to show that you have been listening and are connected with what makes her happy. For an extra response, find the bulbs of her favorite perennial and plant them in the garden as a surprise, letting her know that they are a token of your love and that every time they bloom, they are a sign of how much she means to you. She will be anxiously waiting for them to bloom this year and every year after!

Love Bath. Have a candlelight bubble bath drawn with floating rose petals waiting when she returns home from work. Have a jazz playlist ready on your iPod to enhance the mood. Add a glass of champagne or sparkling wine to provide that additional bit of relaxation. Buy a new, comfortable (yet inexpensive) bathrobe and wrap it with a big red bow. Have it ready when she exits the tub.

Movie Night. Buy or rent two or three chick flicks that women love—her favorite movies would be nice! Buy an inexpensive soft blanket, large enough for two, and wrap it in a red bow (Marshalls or Home Goods is a great place to start). Prearrange a babysitter and surprise her with a movie marathon. (F.Y.I. you need to actually watch the movies with her.)

Lay Hands. Give her a candlelight massage with her favorite mood-enhancing music. Heighten the mood by using aromatherapy body oil or lotion. Focus your efforts on her back, **neck, shoulders, scalp, earlobes, and feet**!

Foot Fetish. Give her a surprise pedicure which includes a **warm soaking foot bath, a scrub with foot brush or pum**-ice stone, foot massage with eucalyptus lotion, and for extra credit, top it off by painting her toenails!

Getaway. Have a stay-cation in town at a local hotel. Find an overnight sitter and tell her in advance to keep the evening free to avoid any work or extracurricular conflicts. **When she arrives home from work, tell her she has 10 minutes to pack a simple overnight bag, hop in the car, and head** to your favorite local hotel.

Comfort Food. Make a reservation at her favorite restaurant, present flowers to her in the car, and open/close her door, if it's a family-owned restaurant, ask if they can prepare one of her favorite dishes as a custom order (probable an added fee).

Prepare a Table. Fix her a surprise dinner (something simple but tasteful unless you are an amazing chef), add fresh-cut flowers to your table setting. Serve the meal using **your wedding china and stemware, and eat together** by candlelight with soft music.

Chef's Choice. Hire a local chef to prepare a gourmet candlelight meal for the two of you (reputable students from your local culinary school can be considered). While dinner is being expertly prepared, engage her with meaningful conversation, inquire about her day, and get engaged with whatever may be on her mind. Try listening instead of talking.

Dance Fever. When she walks in the door from work, say to her, "May I have this dance?" Have a playlist of favorite love songs ready on your iPod and slow dance the evening away. It will be an extra bonus if you have already sprayed on just a bit of her favorite cologne. Be sure to kiss her forehead and eyelids while dancing. These types of kisses feel more protective and adds to an overall display of support.

Nightcap. During the day, ask her to make some time later for a "nightcap" without explaining what you mean. Once kids are asleep and you two have some privacy, share chocolate-covered strawberries or strawberries with whipped cream by candlelight. Add some slow music and a glass of champagne. When she asks what you're celebrating, say "Our love."

Healing Hands. Get a couples' massage at a respected spa in the area. Hold hands, kiss, and caress between services.

Vicky's Secret. Buy her new lingerie but keep in mind that many American women over 30 years old perceive some type of flaw in their body image, so avoid lingerie options that are too tight or too short which may make her feel uncomfortable with her figure. Instead, consider a long and slinky nightgown. Have it wrapped in a nice box or package. **For bonus points, add a pair of feathery slipper heels and a** new bottle of perfume.

Play in the Grass. Have a picnic basket prepared with light **fare including cheeses, fruit, crackers, wine, and wine** glasses. Prepare a romantic setting with candlelight in the backyard (on a blanket in the grass or picnic table with fresh flowers). If using chairs, consider adding to the aesthetics by **wrapping the chair backs in white cloth like a formal dinner** or reception. Romantic music is a must. Engage her with stimulating conversation and a listening ear.

Music to Her Ears. If she likes music, hire a local musician **to perform an hour of her favorite love songs in your** home. Dance cheek-to-cheek in the middle of the living room as if no one else is watching.

These small displays of adoration with a romantic twist will help her reclaim her femininity. Help that office stress **melt away by reminding her that she does not have to do it all** when she is with you. Appeal to her softer side and reaffirm **that you are her protector, even when the world convinces** her that she can only depend on herself. Assure her that the **tough armor that she has worn all day at work can be shed** at the door—the home you two share is her safe haven. Con**vince her that sinking into your arms is the safest place on** earth.

Chapter Nine
Damaged Goods

THE FEMALE BREADWINNER ARCHETYPE IN many circumstances can be thought of as the manifestation of successful schooling, ambition, and adequate career preparation. If we think of this type of woman along a continuum: **Before she was married, she was likely a powerhouse** as a single female. She may have been an educated single woman with leadership potential, on a path toward a good career and an impressive salary. You can just imagine her in a sleek designer suit, peep-toe shoes, sitting atop a barstool at a singles mixer looking composed and in control. But how is she being perceived by her potential suitors? Is the high-achieving single female with breadwinner potential seen as a **commodity or damaged goods?**

During the process of writing this book, I found myself becoming more and more cognizant of people's responses once I revealed my book topic in conversation. One evening I **happened to be riding in the car with some friends,** a young couple who lives close by. We were heading out for a nice dinner. I mentioned to the husband, Rick, that my book topic was Female Breadwinners. His response was an exasperated, "Uggggggh!!" So, I shifted in my chair and turned to face him. "Why do you give that response?" I asked. He replied, "I always told myself I would NEVER marry a woman who made more than me!" I was shocked at this response as I had previously **pegged him as a down-to-earth, approachable, and** easy-going type of guy. But that comment stung with chauvinism and judgment of female breadwinners like myself. I responded, "Really? But you're automatically excluding eligible women with whom you could be extremely compatible."

At that moment, I realized that even in today's society, there remains a segment of men who still perceive the high-earning female as an undesirable partner, simply because she has achieved greater financial success. Without getting to know her personality, her likes and dislikes, her goals, or her hobbies—she has already been dismissed. She will be automatically discounted by some male suitors at that singles mixer because she mentioned doctor or judge or CEO in her perfunctory introductory conversation. Despite the more liberal views to which society has become accustomed regarding equality for women, men who think like Rick do still exist.

When an eligible man automatically discounts a woman because of her salary or success, he is treating her as if she is damaged goods. Before he understands the core of who she is and what she has to offer, he will mentally place her in the "discard" pile and move on to the gal at the next barstool. I am not saying that most men act this way, but I am sure this type of guy exists somewhere in your friend circle. Why do some men run from a woman just because she may have great intellect, a wealth of life experiences, and a bigger bank account? These traits should be viewed as a bonus in the dating world when singles assess the benefits that each potential mate is bringing to the table. After all, marriage is a contract. In fact, it is the most serious contract that most of us will ever enter into. So why wouldn't a single man want to enter into a life-long, binding contract with an educated and experienced female? Wouldn't an accomplished woman **enhance his life as much if not even more than a woman with** little or no education or life experiences?

Why is the high-achieving and successful female being punished by some men in the dating world simply because of her accomplishments? Does her salary imply the type of woman that she is? No. Do more zeros at the end of her salary make her any less desirable, any less sexy, any less maternal? No. Or, maybe these attributes make her seem less subordinate and less subservient. Do some eligible men think that she'll have too much ambition or insurmountable self-esteem? **What do those men who shun successful women fear?**

We live in a modern society that is obsessed with the importance of "brand management" in the world of marketing and public relations. My fear is that the brand of the successful single female may be broken. I fear that she has not effectively defined her own brand; therefore, the world, particularly a small subset of insecure men, have developed a brand for her. This is likely fueling common yet undermining myths about her. We've all heard the verbal insults about her like, "She doesn't need a man," or, "She's high maintenance." But as statistics reveal, the type of female that out-earns her mate is becoming the American standard. As mentioned in **Chapter Two: Single, childless women ages 22-30 currently** out-earn their male counterparts in the majority of American cities. As we process these statistics, it becomes clear that the negative connotations often associated with the higher-earning, successful female must be dispelled if the institution **of marriage is to remain viable and desirable moving forward** in the millennium.

A man in search of a compatible mate who makes the **decision to exclude a woman simply because her** salary bracket supersedes his, in my opinion, is acting out of fear and insecurity. There is really no other explanation. In mak**ing a decision to avoid this type of woman, he may be** reacting to a female persona rooted in inaccuracy and falsehood. What this segment of the male population should realize is **that there are many successful women who are longing to be** in a relationship with a man who can act as her leader. And **most of these women will be willing to submit to a man with** such qualities. Chapter Four provided a good overview of the leadership characteristics that this type of woman desires including financial literacy, sacrifice for the household, fairness in acknowledging her attributes, and respect for her as your team mate. If a man possesses these qualities, he will solidify his position as the leader in a relationship with a powerhouse female.

Let me repeat. A single woman with breadwinning potential is NOT damaged goods! Sure, she has an air of confidence and self-assuredness. But she has come by these traits honestly. An adult woman in the millennium has likely been groomed since childhood to be self-sufficient and independent. I know I was. Her father likely taught her to reach for the stars in education because she needn't depend on a man for her survival. Her mother advised her against being "stuck" in a marriage for convenience and security. She has been raised to enjoy the company of a man, but not to necessarily depend on one. Today's single woman is the product of a profound shift in the thinking of the American culture, which has become most evident over the last 40 years.

A quick review of divorce statistics will reveal clues as to why young women of today are taught to be so independent.

In January 1970, the first "no-fault" divorce bill was put into effect by California Governor, Ronald Reagan, which allowed **married couples to separate for almost any reason, or no** reason at all. This new bill essentially eliminated the "legally binding" aspect of a marriage agreement. The result was a **doubling of the divorce rate which reached its peak around** 1981. Approximately half of the children born to married **parents in the 1970s saw their parents split up, compared to** only 11% of those kids born in the 1950s.[1]

As mothers survived divorce, they were forced to find ways to provide for their children through work or education or both. Whether welcomed or not, this sense of independence experienced by a new faction of "ex-wives" has been passed down. For this reason and many others, generations of young girls since then have been taught to be self-sufficient. After all, she may never know when the security of marriage may be swept out from under her.

I challenge men who may be reading this book and may have behaviors consistent with Rick's to take a step back for a second. Do these men have children or plan to have them **one day? How will they advise their daughters regarding** education and how her success will be viewed by her male **counterparts? Will these men teach their daughters to get** a good education and excel in life? Or will they teach these daughters to go far, but just not any farther than the average male because then they'll be afraid of you? Will these **men tell their daughters the honest truth? That if she gets good grades in school, and goes to college, and maybe goes**

---

1 W. Bradford Wilcox, "The Evolution of Divorce," *National Affairs, no.1* (2009), http://www.nationalaffairs.com/publications/detail/the-evolution-of-divorce (accessed July 2012).

to graduate school, and gets a good job, with a high salary—that with each accolade and achievement, she will lose footing with men in her age group because they will see her as damaged goods. Will he tell her candidly that her likelihood of finding a mate will rest on how well she curtails her own success to match the man in front of her?

The profound change in thinking regarding how we raise young girls in this country has resulted in a disconnect. There is a disconnect between what young girls are expected to accomplish according to mom and dad, and what her future boyfriend may desire in his mate. Moms and dads of today expect their daughters to acquire good grades in school. After all, education is paramount, so that she may "take care of herself." Most of today's parents prepare young women for a college education and a successful transition into the work force. The segment of society that grooms young women to depend solely on a husband for money and security still exists, but in much smaller numbers than ever before in American history. So what happens when these young ladies do just as mom and dad said—get the education and the great career and find themselves sitting lonely on a barstool getting passed over by men because of their success?

To these young women, it feels like a cruel joke. It feels like the rug has been pulled out from beneath them. The dreams of success that were cultivated by her parents, and fueled by her teachers, and crafted by her mentors has come back to bite her in the backside. I know countless successful, beautiful, and nurturing females who have failed to find a mate, including some women who are very close to me. Many men and women reading this book can find examples of such ladies in their own network of friends. How is it that the determination and self-reliance that has allowed her to achieve in life now relegates her to the damaged goods category when it comes to love? When asked about what she wants for her own daughter, Breadwinner Monica mentioned: "I want my daughter to be very independent. I want her to go to school but... I don't know what I want from her. I also think that being a high-wage earner may limit her marriage potential." It's just not fair. We, as a society, have got to find a balance; we have got to figure this thing out. The very fabric of the American marriage and the perpetuation of the American family depends on it.

As our nation's singles delay marriage in lieu of education, a young woman's reproductive capacity after marriage is lessening. Today, the average age of first marriage for women is age 27, up from age 20 in 1960.[2] **The females who do find that match made in heaven are already behind the eight-ball with regards to child-rearing capabilities. So, imagine how the powerhouse single woman feels who is struggling to be loved by men, some of whom fear her because of her** success. If we think of the "damaged goods phenomenon" in a genealogical sense, we will see that it has the potential to be much more serious than it initially appears.

If the high-achieving, successful woman is cast aside by male suitors who fail to try understand her, she will not marry. If she does not marry, she may not reproduce; if she **fails to reproduce, she cannot contribute to the gene pool; if she cannot contribute to the gene pool, then her kind will** become extinct. I know this a far-reaching theory, and in say**ing this I risk being compared to the folktale favorite, Chicken** Little, but my analytical mind can't help but to draw such

---

2 16.Stephanie Coontz "Marriage: Saying 'I don't' " *Los Angeles Times*, 19 Jan. 2012, http://www.articles.latimes.com/2012/jan/19/opinion/la-oe-coontz-marriage-20120119 (accessed May 2012).

conclusions if ambitious women continue to be viewed as undesirable by her male counterparts. This scenario would, of course, be a victory for a less ambitious subset of women who may forego education and career. After all, they would be viewed as the cream of the crop to eligible bachelors (this is not meant to belittle stay-at-home moms or homemakers who I recognize have contributed to the very fabric of who we are as a nation). But something tells me that the world would eventually miss the Oprah Winfreys, the Susan B. Anthonys, the Condoleezza Rices, the Janet Renos—**successful single females that did not marry but have changed the world**. So, as a society, we should endeavor ourselves to keep them around and preserve their viability in the gene pool.

I encourage the men reading this book, who are currently walking away from the successful girl in the sleek black suit, to stop for a second and think. **Think about how his daughter will feel when the men that she desires walk away from** her because of her accomplishments. Think of your daughter's pain when she is treated like damaged goods simply for achieving the success that you as her father encouraged. Take the time to recognize and remember that the young lady in front of you is "Daddy's Little Girl" to someone in this world.

A man who refuses to give a woman with breadwinning potential a fair shot is truly missing out. He is missing out on a fulfilling and gratifying relationship with a true helpmeet and partner in life. Men should recognize that a female breadwinner as a wife is not only able to contribute more financially; **but she likely brings a wealth of intellect and life experiences** that can propel that united couple to even greater heights. Naturally, as humans, we fear what we don't understand. The **purpose of this book is to help men understand her so that** they may take advantage of all that she has to offer!

Chapter Ten
You Can't Eat Love for Dinner

THERE HAS BEEN A SHIFT in the age appropriateness of marriage in a modern society that is grossly different from past generations. During my parents' era, in the 1950s and '60s, some high school sweethearts married soon after 12th grade. They didn't know their "heads from a hole in the wall" and barely had two pennies between them. These young couples fell crazy in love, got married, maybe **found a small house with help from their parents, and started** their lives together. They worked toward something and built a life together. In addition to building a life, they were building a bank account. Babies ensued soon after marriage and **many wives chose to stay home with the kids, possibly** having small jobs that required little to no education. Back then, **the average husband and wife started from nothing and grew** something together.

Fast forward to today. Couples marrying right out of high school is almost unheard of. American adolescents are advised to pursue college first, then marriage, then babies. **Nowadays, a young woman who conceives a child at 18 years** old, even if she decides to marry, is pitied. Some in society may believe that "her life is over" as she missed out on her opportunity to go to college and make a better life for herself. Today's expectations are much higher for women to "make their own way" before settling down with a man. A young woman is taught to get good grades, secure an education, and get a job to support herself. No longer are parents advising young women to "find a good man to take care of you." These women are told to stand on their own two feet FIRST and then find a suitable mate. More often than not, today's **women are expected to complete undergraduate school, and** maybe even graduate school, before settling down and starting a family. Once women and men are preoccupied with the **demands of academia, it is less likely that they will place a** priority on marriage at that particular time in their lives.

In a modern world, marriage feels more *rational* once the goal of education is accomplished. Today's youth view marriage as a milestone that is best pursued after gaining stability and a steady income. So, how has this trend affected women's approach to love and marriage? Well, first off, the **average woman is of a more mature age when she starts to** seriously consider marriage. As mentioned in the previous chapter, the median age at first marriage in 2010 for females was 27 years of age versus 20 years of age in 1960. This **seven-year delay in marriage may have allowed these women to** complete undergraduate education, or graduate school, or they may have secured a job and subsequent income. If she **has been working for a few years, even at the age of 27 years,** she may have some form of savings or investments. Once **she reaches her 30s and 40s, she may have accumulated a** substantial financial nest egg before saying "I do." How is the courtship of modern couples affected by more financially **secure single women?**

Female breadwinner, Teresa, admitted in her interview **that she had been taken advantage of in the past by two ex-**husbands who callously ran through her money. She sacrificed finance for romance, and the resulting turmoil landed her in the poor house. After her second divorce, she worked hard, maximized her career in education, and retired with decent money and stability. She was determined and steadfast and found a way to recover from those financial setbacks that had been cloaked in a facade of "love." She *needs* to be **financially secure as she moves forward toward the golden years** of retirement. In addition, she has adult children to whom she wants to leave a little something when she's gone. **Although Teresa has found a man that she loves who asked for** her hand in marriage, she refuses to marry him. Teresa has made a decision to avoid the financial vulnerability of such a union at this point in her life.

If you liken this concept to common practices regarding **investments and the stock market—the older you become,** the less risky your investments should be. When she was **younger, Teresa took a risk on a man who said he loved her** but left her with nothing, forcing her to rely on food stamps. The second husband, although initially the breadwinner, lost a good job due to irresponsible behavior, and ran through their money. She was forced to move back home with her parents after her finances were reduced to nothing. Both men stole her financial security like bandits in the night. Teresa had taken on financial risks for the sake of love in her past relationships and got burned, not once—but twice!

Now that she is older, the financial vulnerability that accompanies marriage is far too risky for her at this juncture in her life. She cannot afford to make frivolous mistakes now that she has entered her retirement years. This female **breadwinner is willing to forego marriage altogether if it means that she must share her greatest assets: her home, her in-**vestment portfolio, and her cash savings. Her past experiences have taught her that she must "protect" herself from the man whom she now loves. In her interview, Teresa stated, "We were engaged but I called off the engagement. It was partly financial. He wanted to put his name on the house that I just bought. And I wasn't going to do that. It didn't protect all my 37 years of teaching and education—so I called it off. **If we get married, it opens all my assets to community property—everything to a 50/50 split and I'm just not doing that.**" In her mind, she cannot fully trust another man with her financial welfare. According to Teresa, it is safer to forego love for financial stability, because you can't eat love for dinner.

So, how does one separate finance from romance? **Should marriage be perceived as a type of business deal or investment?** Indeed, it is. But society tells us that prenuptial **agreements and other such prearranged exit strategies are so** unromantic. But if your first two spouses leave you in financial **ruin, and you turn around and approach the third relationship in the same manner, not only are you risking poverty in retirement, Suzie Orman would say you're insane! But on the other hand, how can her current boyfriend feel trusted,** loved, and respected if he is not allowed to share her "space" financially? I can imagine that would leave him feeling shut out and dejected; he exists outside of her "circle of trust." Such feelings are indeed understandable and may be difficult for him to digest. However, men facing this circumstance **must ask themselves if *their* actions have also fueled her feelings of insecurity?**

This tough question requires an extraordinary amount of introspection, but it's worth working through it to get to the root of Teresa's concerns. Has her current boyfriend shown fiscal irresponsibility during the courtship and engagement?

Has he failed to display financial leadership in their relationship, i.e. poor credit scores, failure to pay bills on time, financial dependence on others to purchase large ticket items (co-signer, co-borrower), failure to set and keep financial goals **for himself or the household, inability to budget money** properly, having overdrawn bank accounts, showing little or no retirement savings, rainy day funds, or emergency funds? ALL of these behavior patterns make it very difficult for a woman to trust you with her hard-earned assets.

Breadwinner Cicely acknowledged this by saying, "If **people are not responsible with their money, then they are not going to be responsible with** *your* money. If your credit score is 500 and mine is 700, then we are not having a joint account." This statement may imply that for a financially savvy woman of the millennium, the fear of financial ruin super**sedes any biblical or cultural advice she may have received to** combine monies after marriage.

If a man appears financially illiterate to a stable, career-minded female breadwinner, it will be difficult for her to trust him with her financial well-being. Without such reassurance, she is likely to separate the two of your coffers and act as an independent with regards to finances over the years in your marriage. It's your choice. This is one instance in life where you MUST lead by example. Otherwise, your female breadwinner will inherently take the lead. You may feel relieved at first to shed the responsibilities of financial leadership in your marriage; but ultimately, you may resent this behavior over time. I am not implying that such a hierarchy with the female as the lead can't be successful, that is a couple's individual choice. But it can present itself as a challenge to a subset of men who will eventually regret this loss of financial control in their marriages.

Solid finances are very important to most female breadwinners. She feels good about her ability to provide for her family, it becomes part of her identity. In a previous chapter, **we discussed that the female breadwinner has a dual identity**—her career identity, which reaps the finances, and her identity at home as a wife and mother. Based on the interviews, both of these identities seem to be important components of who she is. This became evident in the interviews **when the women were asked if they would leave their ca**reers behind if it were causing their marriages to suffer due to her husband's damaged ego. The overwhelming majority of female breadwinners I interviewed answered no. They can **leave their careers behind for love, but not solely to pacify** her husband's ego.

Many breadwinners responded that they have worked hard to get to where they are today, in both education and career. This suggests that their accomplishments in these areas have helped to make them who they are today. Annette responded, "I would not leave my job. I have too much invested. I only have two more years before I can retire." Annette has put in the time in her career and has the accomplishments to show for it. The financial security of retirement is something that she has earned; she is not willing to prioritize her mate's emotional needs over finance. She will not sacrifice years of career accomplishment for an irrational reason such as a bruised ego.

Breadwinner Melissa had a similar response to the idea of prioritizing her husband's ego over career and finance. "I would not dumb down my income for him. That's his problem. He would need to figure out what he needs to do. If a promotion stopped me from having quality time with my

family, *then* I would probably turn down that promotion, but not because of his insecurities." Melissa was not alone. All but **one female breadwinner was in accordance with this think**ing. This implies that the female breadwinner sees career and financial security as an important part of her identity. And this is a part of her identity that she plans to maintain.

In addition to providing that sense of identity, career and finance also affords a woman more security and leverage in the marriage. By having such leverage, it is less likely that she **will be disenfranchised by her husband regarding the deci**sion-making of the marriage. She will be in a position to contribute more to the running of the household if she desires.

Breadwinner Francine admitted, "I would love it if [my daughter] could find someone who was rich. But I don't want her to be disempowered. I don't want her to be overly dependent on a man."

But there was one interviewee, Donna, who *was* **willing** to prioritize her husband's ego over her money and career. She believed that "a woman should do everything she can for her partner." For Donna, there was no connection made between her career identity and her financial security within the context of her marriage. "I went from $37 an hour to a minimum-wage job hoping it would save the marriage. When I look back at it, I'm sorry I did that because now I'm trying to still get back into my profession and it's harder now for me to get back on top. The husband ran. So I'm just stuck financially."

Donna tried to do what she felt was "right" as a wife in placing her husband's needs before her own as it relates to **love** *and* finance. Sadly, things in her marriage didn't turn out as she had hoped. Her husband was not willing to reciprocate by putting *her* needs before his, which is the gamble that we take in love. In retrospect, Donna wishes that she had taken a more pragmatic approach to the marriage by recognizing that her financial security should have been just as much of a priority as his emotional needs.

The importance of financial security to a female breadwinner should not be interpreted as a display of selfishness. **It has more to do with a sense of helplessness when it comes to affairs of the heart.** A woman will inherently feel like she is losing control when she gives herself to a man, particularly if he fails to inspire confidence regarding his financial prowess. So it's no surprise that this process of marriage can be especially daunting for a successful woman who knows her worth and values. She may be apprehensive about placing her hard-earned coffers into the hands of someone else. Love **is not based on logic; the person you fall in love with may be** qualified to be your leader but it's not a guarantee.

So how do you place all your confidence in someone just because you "love" him, but you are unsure if he is qualified for this all-important position? This is where trust has **to come into play—and as we all know, some people can be** trusted and some just can't. So if she decides to say, "I do," she has to trust that this man will cultivate their combined finances, helping it to grow like a farmer with his harvest. But there are no guarantees in love. The wrong man can easily squander that money away to nothing. So, in this sense, the choice to marry becomes an intimidating decision, to say the least.

The reality is that this decision to marry affects far more than just the monies she has accumulated prior to marriage; it has the potential to affect her credit, her debt profile, retirement savings patterns, and many other aspects of her financial well-being. When women were asked if they would leave **their careers behind to save their marriages, the** overwhelming majority said NO. The one woman who adamantly said YES ended up alone and financially destitute. She made the ultimate sacrifice for her marriage and she paid the ultimate price. I am not advocating that women put money before love BUT I am advocating that we "look out for ourselves" enough to maintain financial solvency in case he decides to leave now or in the future. This approach is particularly necessary for a mature woman who has more to lose and less time to recover before retirement. Unless a man can prove that he is worthy in more ways than one, some of today's women may **decide to pass on this complex business arrangement called** marriage. "Cause you can't eat love for dinner!"

Chapter Eleven
The Covenant: The Virtue of Fairness

WHEN A HUSBAND AND WIFE come together in a blessed union, the endearing concept of love is frequently placed as the primary bond of a healthy relationship. But there are many other components of a successful union which, if left unaddressed, will challenge any relationship that love has brought together. One of **those crucial components is the teamwork and partnership necessary for the successful running of a household and family.** This partnership should be thought of like a "covenant" or promise. Husband and wife come together as one before God and pledge to care for one another, for better, for worse, for richer, for poorer, in sickness, and in health. That promise or **covenant that a couple entered into on their wedding day, at** the exchange of their vows, requires them to function as one **unit, regardless of the circumstances that may arise in the** marriage. This concept of partnership becomes *profoundly* important to a female breadwinner.

The woman of the household, potentially operating as wife and mother, traditionally assumes the role of **Head Caregiver** of the household, right? This may include keeping hot food on the table; keeping the domicile clean and organized; keeping the kids, the husband, and the dog on track and otherwise satisfied. So, what happens when the day comes when **Head Caregiver** of the household must also step into the position of **Head Earner** of the household? Over time, some of her responsibilities as **Head Caregiver** will invariably begin to suffer. It's just a matter of time. And if you haven't witnessed her being less attentive to some of those caregiver duties, then quite frankly she is probably miserable because **she is doing too much!**

Let's think of the covenant or promise of a marriage as we would a colorful pie chart with the wife's duties shaded in pink and the husband's duties shaded in blue. Together, the pink and blue shaded portions of the pie chart make up a whole. Of course, I recognize that in any marriage, duties or responsibilities are often skewed in one person's favor for many reasons. But let's use a 50/50 split as the model to which we should all assert ourselves. When the wife assumes **the role of breadwinner, regardless of the reason, she is assuming one of the traditionally blue duties of the pie chart. So, as she steps in to fill that space, whether she wants to or not, regardless of which life circumstances have dictated** this change, she is taking on a pretty hefty blue duty. As her partner in a union created before God, her husband should be willing to reciprocate and assume one of the duties previously shaded in pink on the pie chart.

Depending on the couple's household dynamics, the **husband may have to assume the new duty of chef, or laun**dry professional, or housekeeper, or caregiver for the kids. I **understand that in many cases, both husband and wife are** sharing the duty of wage-earner. Therefore, I am certainly not attempting to belittle the husband's contribution to the financial well-being of the home! But the wife's role as breadwinner, especially if it's a new circumstance, likely comes with extra responsibilities and stressors which may make her less

The Covenant: The Virtue of Fairness | 241

available for a few of her pink duties on the pie chart. These responsibilities could include filling in extra hours at the office, more work-related travel, bringing more work home from the office, engaging in more conference calls after work hours, working late into the night resulting in sleep deprivation and fatigue, and the list goes on. Sometimes despite her best efforts, she simply can't keep up a particular task with the same diligence.

In her interview, Breadwinner Sharon described that she is not embarrassed about being the sole breadwinner in her marriage, but what she is embarrassed about is that she has to "go out and work a 9-5 and then come home and still do *all* the traditional things." She says, "If I had a husband who said, 'I'm not going to work, but when you come home, dinner is going to be ready and the house is gonna be clean,' [then I would be happy]. But you're out playing golf every day, and I still have to cook dinner, wash clothes, the house is a wreck, and I still have to do all the traditional roles." Sadly, after several years of this behavior, her husband's unwillingness to uphold the covenant lead to the demise of their marriage.

I am sensitive to the fact that the decision for a man to take on some of his wife's duties once his salary is surpassed may result in feelings of resentment, particularly if such duties are perceived as "domestic" or "womanly" duties. However, if he uses a rational approach as the head of household, the proper functioning of the family should always be the priority. As the leader of the household, he must recognize **that despite this new circumstance of his wife as the female** breadwinner, the pie chart hasn't changed. And to keep his castle running smoothly as she shifts into a huge new duty, someone has to fill that pink-shaded position which is now empty. His wife simply can't do it all! Breadwinner Cicely mentioned, "The energy that could have been spent between husband and wife at night time has been spent with the breadwinner having to do additional duties like cooking, cleaning, etc. So, then, the woman is tired. [Too tired for sex and intimacy.]"

This concept of upholding the covenant should surpass any hang-ups regarding which tasks belong to which gender. **For example, think of an able-bodied man who enters into** a marriage with a woman and then he unexpectedly suffers from a back injury resulting in long-term immobility. Despite his best efforts, he simply can no longer fulfill some of his blue duties on the pie chart. In such a scenario, his wife as his life partner is naturally expected to step in and fill that void. She will begin to carry out more labor-intensive duties that **were previously his responsibility, like shoveling snow in the** winter, carrying the family's luggage, or mowing the lawn. That is a sign of her love for him and her dedication to upholding the covenant of their marriage... doing what it takes **to make the family and the household whole**.

I would hope that any husband, acting as the leader in the marriage, would be able to put his ego aside for the betterment of his family. He should be willing to be a team player, fill in the blanks, and pick up the pieces. That is the only way **that the covenant can be successful; each partner is willing to** do whatever it takes to keep that pie chart whole and in tact. It is not productive for the husband to simply sit back and watch his wife struggle to juggle her position as top wage-earner and still try to tackle all the pink duties on the pie chart. Over time, she will spread herself too thin and will not **only become miserable but may be overcome with feelings of** inadequacy. She needs your help! She needs you to support her by recognizing that a shift in duties has occurred; there are portions of the pie chart that now need your attention. Your willingness to take on one of her previous duties will be perceived as true dedication to her and to your household. Breadwinner Helen summed it up nicely: "You can't be chief breadwinner and top bottle washer, too. It's just a matter of time [before it all falls apart]."

As the head of household, it should be your priority to ensure a healthy balance of responsibilities in the household and in the marriage. Upholding the covenant is the first step. By assuming one of your wife's more domestic duties, **you will have shown that the success and well-being of your** household is paramount. You will have prioritized your family, **despite the internal struggle that you may be experiencing** regarding gender-based associations with household roles. Your marriage, your wife, and your entire family will be better off because of it.

Chapter Twelve
Sow Your Seeds: The Virtue of Financial Literacy

SO A MAN FINDS HIMSELF in love with a woman who earns more. So now what? Should he feel sorry for himself and wallow in regret? Should he begin questioning his worth in the marriage? Should he feel that he has lost control of his family and household? Absolutely NOT! A very successful approach to such a marriage is to see the shared income of the household as only a starting point. The wife's higher income provides only a foundation; there is plenty of potential for financial growth with a knowledgeable and faithful husband at the helm. What I mean by this statement is that husbands of female breadwinners should approach the shared funds of the marriage as "seed money" that can be cultivated and grown with his initiative and expertise. The husband of a female breadwinner should consider approaching his monthly household surplus as a farmer would approach seeds to be sown in preparation for a harvest.

This approach may be even more beneficial for marriages in which the wife's income surpasses the husband's by a large degree. This husband may initially feel as if his income and thus his financial contribution to the marriage are expendable. This feeling may cause him to question his overall value or worth in the marriage. If his income is dwarfed by his wife's income, psychologically, he may struggle with how to financially claim a stake in the marriage. How does he begin to feel that he has some ownership in the family's monetary worth?

For starters, one should refrain from equating "earned income" with one's "financial contribution" to the marriage because the two are not mutually exclusive. A man's financial contribution to the marriage and to the household can far exceed his earned income. Men married to a female breadwinner have not only the ability, but also the duty to contribute to the financial solvency of the marriage. This can be approached in several ways. He can contribute *intellectually* by developing a sound financial plan for the family including monthly household budgeting, college savings, emergency fund, retirement savings, etc. By establishing himself as the financial leader in the marriage, he is contributing to the solidarity of the family, moving them on a path toward greater wealth.

Breadwinner Teresa stated, "[Husbands] have to become financially educated so they can make investments, do savings, and make out a financial plan for the family. [If my husband can help] the family stick to the plan and gain financial independence, I would be highly grateful and respectful. A man who says these are our goals and sees that the family sticks to it, leads the way."

A second approach that husbands of female breadwinners can consider is the provision of a *fiscal* contribution beyond that of his earned income. He should challenge himself to explore smart investment channels that will help his wife's earned income flourish over time. Such investments could include stock, bonds, real estate, or entrepreneurship. But this can only be accomplished once a man begins to think beyond the boundaries of his earned income as his sole contribution to the marriage. Once the husband of a female breadwinner establishes financial leadership, he has indeed claimed a stake in the finances of the marriage. By sowing the financial **seeds of his household, he has provided added value to the** household's wealth, as opposed to feeling like an appendage which can be hard for any man to endure.

For example, let's say that the husband of a female bread**winner chooses to explore a sound real estate investment** that fits within the household budget. The couple may intend to flip a reasonably-priced property over a moderate period of time, or may choose to become long-term landlords. When approached judiciously and with patience, real estate investing can still be a sound long-term investment despite the struggling economy. If a husband can position himself now as **an educated landlord, he can ensure viable passive income** for the entire family in the future. Even though the husband may not be making the bulk of the "earned income" in the marriage, he has taken the joint seed money and has helped it to grow. Alternatively, after appropriate research and plan**ning, husbands can consider entrepreneurship to generate** passive household income and increase wealth. This is the approach that my husband and I took in my own marriage. Regardless of the strategy used, if a husband pursues a series of financially savvy investments over the course of the marriage, he has the potential to help the family's financial pot grow. This pot has the potential to flourish into something **much greater than his female breadwinner would have ever** accomplished without his assistance.

The reason this concept of "sowing seeds" becomes so **important to female breadwinners is that many women feel** that once she reaches breadwinner status in the marriage, some husbands choose to relinquish financial control of the household over to her. This may be done willingly, because he no longer feels like being bothered; or may be done begrudgingly, because he thinks that this is indeed what his wife wants. The latter assumption is usually incorrect. A female breadwinner who seems to want control of the finances may be operating in "rescue mode." She may see a lack of financial drive or competency in her mate, and may feel compelled to take over this responsibility. Remember our recurring theme: If a female breadwinner sees areas of inadequacy in the home or in the marriage, she will step in and take over. But she may do so resentfully.

There were many instances throughout the interviews when the wife felt alone at the helm in running the finances of the marriage. In Breadwinner Monica's opinion, "The person who withstands the financial pressures of the household is, in essence, the head of household or leader." I cannot argue with that conclusion. She feels that she has been placed at the helm of the financial decision-making because she is the breadwinner. "It's a lot of pressure and I don't want the pressure. I know he doesn't perceive it that way."

The husbands of female breadwinners need to understand that they can still remain the financial leader in the marriage. In fact, his wife will likely prefer this scenario as long as he's competent at it. He should commit to staying involved in the day-to-day finances of the family including monthly budget, bill-paying responsibilities, tax preparation, long-term investments, etc. He should not just "check-out" of the situation once his income is surpassed. But instead, he should be present, active, and in charge of the financial well-being of the marriage and family.

If the husband of a breadwinner does decide to "checkout" mentally with regards to the finances, his wife may begin to feel resentful that she is left with the sole burden of maintaining financial solvency in the household. It may feel like she is being dumped on, just another duty for her to tackle unilaterally, without the support or assistance from her husband.

In Breadwinner Cicely's case, her husband's income fluctuated based on a monthly commission. She felt that when her husband would come up short in the finances in a particular month, she would be left to pick up the pieces and figure out how to make ends meet that month. She resented feeling caught off guard when the finances were low. Cicely commented, "Sometimes I feel like, 'What if I don't have it? You just depend on me. What happens when my week doesn't work out?' I have periods of resentment. He depends on me if things fall through for him. I don't feel like I can depend on him if the tables are turned."

Ultimately, such behavior can lead to feelings of mistrust regarding the handling of joint finances. Some husbands may get comfortable with the benefits of having a female breadwinner as a mate, particularly if there is a large income differential. He may feel that if his salary is dwarfed by his wife's salary, then his income is expendable. If he begins to consistently make unilateral decisions about his money without including his wife in the planning, she may begin to feel unsupported, disrespected, and taken advantage of. Breadwinner Gina remarked, "He'll make statements about something he wants to do and then just do it, [although] it has a financial impact. I'm [still] thinking it's in the planning stage and he has already followed through with it. I think he thinks I have more money than I really do."

If feelings of mistrust do begin to develop regarding the handling of finances, it can eventually result in the couple's decision to become financially divergent with regards to bank accounts. Many of the female breadwinners interviewed for this book had chosen the option of separate bank accounts in their marriages. Mostly, this resulted from an overall sentiment of financial irresponsibility displayed in their mates. Because as I mentioned in an earlier chapter, the female breadwinner *will not* **let her ship sink like the Titanic at the hands** of her husband or anyone else for that matter. If his reckless financial behavior is placing the family's financial viability at risk, she may pursue avenues to remove him from the financial equation. Breadwinner Gina commented, "Initially, we handled things jointly, but now we have assigned bills, because we handle things differently. I don't even put money in the joint account anymore." She made a conscious decision to limit her liability by separating bills into "hers and his" categories. Whether real or perceived, she may feel more protected and removed from a financial shortfall if he comes up short at any given time.

A sense of mistrust and lack of dependability with finances can fester over time and deteriorate the bond between husband and wife. If the female breadwinner begins to feel **as though she has to be the controller of the purse strings because her mate is irresponsible, she may begin to perceive** him as a dependent rather than a partner or leader. This psychological association of seeing the husband as a child or dependent has long-term deleterious affects on the marital dynamics. It has the potential to pervade other aspects of the marriage outside the bank account including sexual intimacy and trust. He may feel more disempowered than ever and she feels more resentful than ever. These two psychological polarities in conjunction are disastrous! Her resentment for **her husband compels her to treat him even more like a child, and her child-like treatment of him makes him act *more* like a child!**

Breadwinner Emma admitted, "We were on vacation, and we saw some things we wanted so I just went ahead and bought them for him. I didn't give him the money because he is financially irresponsible. We had a joint credit card at one time but he didn't know how to handle it so I closed the account." Emma is behaving more like a mother than a wife. Regardless of the circumstances that lead to this point, she has been conditioned to control the purse strings in their marriage.

Feelings of financial dependency can be difficult for any person in a marriage to endure, regardless of the gender. The husbands of female breadwinners may feel as if their financial contribution and worth in the marriage is dampened by a lower salary. This does not have to be the case. If husbands make a conscious choice to remain engaged in the financial **well-being of the household, they can prevent such feelings** of dependency from developing. By providing financial lead**ership and long-term guidance for the family, these husbands** have staked a greater claim in the marital finances. This will not only result in a sense of greater contribution, ownership, **and worth for the husband, but will also provide the needed support that his female breadwinner longs for in the marriage.**

Chapter Thirteen
Do the Hustle:
The Virtue of Sacrifice

FEMALE BREADWINNER DESCRIBES THE NEWEST category of American wife. The women interviewed for this book represent an assorted group of women from different ethnic groups, age brackets, and socio-economic backgrounds. Despite this diversity, there appeared to be a common personality trait among them. These ladies exude a certain assertiveness and ambition that felt very familiar to me, as well. I am not sure which came first, the chicken or the egg, but the female breadwinners showcased here seem to know exactly what they want out of life and have no reservations in going after it. Most of these ladies have achieved some degree of career success, thereby securing breadwinner status in her marriage. The majority of these females appear determined to make the sacrifices necessary to provide a better life for herself and for her family.

When asked why they got married, most admitted that they married for love, companionship, and to provide a stable foundation for a family. Not one of these ladies mentioned financial security or wealth as her motive. But when we dig deeper into the interviews, we can see that some form of security, work ethic, and enterprise is indeed an important component of what a female breadwinner wants to see in her mate.

The title of this chapter, Do the Hustle, has nothing to do with that famous dance from the 1970s, but has everything to do with the level of "get-up-and-go" that female breadwinners desire to see in their mates. "Hustle" is a modern day colloquialism used to describe a person's drive and ambition, particularly as it relates to generating income or furthering one's enterprise or business. Whether they know it or not, some husbands of female breadwinners are being evaluated according to how much "hustle" they bring to the marriage.

Couples fall in love for a myriad of reasons. Partners in a marriage may have personality traits that complement one another, with one spouse naturally over-compensating in an area where the other is weak. On the contrary, other partners in a marriage may have similar personality traits, resulting in a harmonious synergy between them. Regardless of which characteristics brought them together, the uncustomary circumstance of a higher-earning wife in the marriage may begin to challenge some of the traits and ideals that were initially acceptable in the marriage.

For instance, a man who is laid-back and easy-going at the outset of the relationship may seem very desirable to a high-powered single female. While dating, she may see him as a welcomed complement to her high-strung, Type A personality. This young man may seem like the perfect partner to counteract the tension and stress that she tends to find around every corner. He may feel easy and safe to her, providing the balance she needs to offset her fast-paced life and career. But I am not certain if a mate who lacks assertive energy will sustain that female breadwinner for the life of the marriage. Based on my interviews, many female breadwinners desire their husbands to have as much if not *more* drive than she does.

Breadwinning wives tend to value ambition and sacrifice as a sign of "hustle." She needs to see that her mate can match or exceed her drive and stamina. If she has secured a good education, she likely desires him to have secured a decent education as well. If she works long hours, she may want to see that same level of dedication in him (of course, as long as the family and children are accounted for). If she works overtime, she wants to see him "hustle" and work over-time hours, as well. It is as if even in a modern world, **where equality for women feels commonplace, the female** breadwinner still desires the male gender to "out-do" her accomplishments. There is a part of her that wants to see a bit **of cowboy persona in her husband, always rising to the chal**lenge, and never outdone. She wants her husband to rise to the occasion when it comes to career, education, and unconditional sacrifice for the family. She wants her achievements and sacrifices for the family to be surpassed by her husband as the leader. Internally, the dogma of the female breadwinner may be "whatever I can do, he should do better."

When asked how she feels about being the female breadwinner, Monica answered, "I feel a little resentful. I have a full-time job and I have an extra job that I love. I leave [my full-time job] in time to pick our children from school because that is important to me. Then I go home and do stay-at-home Mom stuff, then I work from 7:00 to 11:00 p.m., and he is just enjoying life. He is working, but I feel if I am "hustling" then he should be "hustling." He has the ability to earn what I am earning, so he should go do it." Clearly, Monica wants her efforts as the breadwinner to be matched or surpassed by her husband. Whether right or wrong, she is interpreting her husband's enterprises, whatever they may be, as less ambitious than hers. She is sacrificing her leisure time, as well as her sleep, by taking on an extra home-based job in the evenings. Her personal sacrifice for the family's financial well-being feels very tangible to her. She does not see the same sacrifice or "hustle" in her mate and she is disappointed about that.

The female breadwinner doesn't care so much about the zeros on the end of her man's salary as she does about the blood, sweat, and tears that it took him to achieve it. If the **breadwinner begins to feel that she is pulling more weight in the marriage, not only with regards to salary, but also in** the effort put forth for the household, feelings of resentment become more common. Breadwinner Gina admitted to being regretful that her husband had failed to display more hustle in the area of education. She described, "I've worked very hard to get to this point and I've made the sacrifices. In addition, I went back to school to get a second degree. He decided it wasn't worth the time. [I am resentful because] I can't make the choices I want to make. At the age I am now, I would like to work part-time and be able to cruise into retirement, but I can't afford to do that being the major breadwinner." Gina is at a point in her life where she would like to decrease her career commitments as she nears retirement. She feels that her husband's past decisions to forego further education has hampered her ability to ease into her golden years in the manner that she would like.

Education is only one component of the "hustle" that breadwinners desired to see in their mates. Annette, who is in the midst of divorce, expressed a desire to see her husband's ef**forts match hers with regards to extra work hours and overtime.** "Well, in reference to finances, if he would work as hard as I would, [we would be better off]. I don't think he worked as hard as he could have. I would work a 12-hour shift then go work another four hours—a 16-hour day. Then come home and take care of the kids and the house. I felt if he could have put in as much work as I did then we could have survived."

Some female breadwinners want their husbands to go above and beyond the call of duty as a show of solidarity in the marriage. Some want their husbands to take on "extra" of *something* **in exchange for her being relegated into the breadwinner position.** It seems that some women seek a type of trade-off, as if to say, "I am working hard as the bread**winner, so you need to be working hard doing** *something* **enterprising and productive."**

Breadwinner Sharon described a desire to see her husband be more willing to sacrifice his ego for the family during his long period of unemployment. "For me a spouse is someone who is down for you and truly has your back. It means being Mr. Mom if you have to be or taking a substitute teacher job that you don't really want but it helps to provide for your family. To have the flexibility to do whatever you have **to do for your family without having pride and ego get in the** way. [He should have been willing to start] digging ditches or whatever so he can take care of his family. He just didn't have that drive. I really expected that he would do anything to keep his family afloat." Sharon witnessed her husband turn down jobs during his years of unemployment. He was too proud to sacrifice for his family by finding some form of income to assist his wife during this difficult period, even if it wasn't the perfect job. She expected him to show more "hustle" by taking whatever employment he could find, instead of turning his nose up at jobs that he felt were beneath him.

To many female breadwinners, sacrifice and drive go hand-in-hand when it comes to defining "hustle." Breadwinners do expect their mates to make some sacrifices or compromises to keep the family's needs met and keep them moving in a forward direction. Melissa admitted some degree of **regret that her husband chose a career path that** was less ambitious but brought him greater joy and fulfillment. In ex**change, he was receiving a lower salary than** what his skill set could potentially provide. She felt that his decision to do so was preventing her from spending more time with their children in the role of stay-at-home mom. "So I get frustrated because I want to be able to spend more time with the kids. I wanna work part time or I want to take time off from work— **maybe one or two years—knowing that I can go back into the** work force. But when that conversation comes up, it's almost not entertained because he doesn't want to do anything different from what he's doing now." Whether wrong or right, a part of her wishes that his "hustle" would compel him to sacrifice his own joy and career fulfillment for the betterment of the family.

One thing that became clear to me in the interviews is that there is an undercurrent of competition in some marriages containing a female breadwinner. But in this unique type of competition, the breadwinner *wants* **to see her op**ponent win. She wants to be out-matched by her mate in the areas of ambition, drive, and sacrifice. I am not saying that these expectations are fair, I am simply revealing what may lie beneath the surface in the breadwinner's psyche. When two people enter into a union, there are certain expectations **that are expressed at the commencement of the marriage** and certain others that rise to the surface over time. A female breadwinner's desire to see matching "hustle" in her mate may indeed be one of those expectations that catches her off guard. Although it may lie dormant at the outset of the marriage, **the interviews reveal that this desire can reach a place** of chief importance later on in the marriage.

Chapter Fourteen
Mantrum: The Man Tantrum

HUSBANDS OF FEMALE BREADWINNERS MAY experience many unfamiliar emotions during the course of a marriage to a higher-earning wife. Such emotions may include lowered self-esteem, emasculation, disempowerment, frustration, and regret. Upon reading testimonies from **female breadwinners in this book, it becomes quite clear** that effective communication within these marriages is often lacking—sometimes to a greater degree than a traditional couple. If the husbands of female breadwinners are not able to express themselves effectively to their wives, and fail to recognize a support system outside the marriage, they can begin to feel very alienated and frustrated. If these frustrations remain bottled up, with no form of healthy expression, they may manifest in an unhealthy demonstration of emotions that I call man tantrums or "Mantrums."

I apologize if this chapter title is offensive to the men reading this book. But the term "mantrum" seemed so befitting to describe the ways in which some husbands ineffectively express feelings of disempowerment. These detrimental forms of behavior may indicate some degree of maladjustment on **the part of the husband in dealing with the circumstance of** a female breadwinner. The mantrums that were revealed in **the interviews were varied including verbal insults, passive-**

aggressive behavior, depression, infidelity, and physical aggression. No matter the form of expression, these types of **behavior are detrimental to the marital bond and can have** lasting negative psychological effects for the wife. A few common behavior patterns became evident in the interviews. Did **you catch them?**

Some of mantrums displayed were in the form of verbal insults propagated by the husband, targeting his wife's perceived financial prowess. These comments may be purposefully hurtful to the wife; after all, misery loves company. If the husband is hurting on the inside because he feels disempowered, he may lash out with stinging comments toward his wife. A part of him wants her to hurt, too.

Breadwinner Donna described a time when they visited a **marriage counselor and her husband commented on her at**tentiveness to their daughter. "You are a hell of a mother, but you are not much of a wife." Donna felt that she was doing **everything in her power to keep her marriage strong and via**ble, despite her husband's displeasure with her breadwinner status. Donna's husband had a very difficult time adjusting to his new reality of having a higher-earning wife. She felt that **she had gone to great lengths to placate her husband and** assuage his damaged ego. But she could never do enough to satisfy him. The intent of her husband's comment was not **only to hurt Donna, but also to invoke feelings of inadequacy** in his wife. This was likely done in an attempt to mirror his own feelings of inadequacy about failing to be the provider.

Other husbands chose a passive-aggressive approach to expressing frustration, by engaging in a set of "resistance" behaviors. Teresa's fiancé would frequently fail to put his fair share of money into the joint account for household bills. She remarked, "It's kind of a punishment from him for me not putting his name on my house." Using this approach, the man **exerts control by choosing or not choosing to put money in** their joint account on any given month. She is beholden to him in this regard which he may feel is empowering. Teresa's fiancé also chose a pattern of resistance behavior when he purchased a vacation for the couple but refused to purchase a matching first-class plane ticket for her. She sat in coach. Breadwinner Donna's husband used threats of resistant behavior while in divorce proceedings. He warned her against asserting claims to their estate or else "he [would] not walk [his] daughter down the aisle when she gets married."

Passive-aggression can often be linked back to a previous situation wherein a person's right to anger was not allowed to surface. Emma's husband had experienced a two-year period of unemployment during which time his wife covered the household expenses. She had to make tough choices to make ends meet during that time of economic turmoil in their marriage; she ended up owing back taxes to the IRS. When her husband did finally secure employment, she asked for assistance with the IRS debt. He refused to help, remarking that "when he was unemployed, [she] wouldn't give him $20." His response indicated that he was, in essence, carrying out a vendetta fueled by feelings of disempowerment from a situation that had happened some time ago.

Mantrums can also include expressions of self-pity, self-loathing, depression, and withdrawal, particularly if the husband has experienced a loss of employment. Although irrational, some men equate self-worth with gainful employment and career. Donna's husband made a very pitiful statement when he first noticed that her weekly salary surpassed his.

"Take the baby and run; you don't need me!" This statement **implies that in his mind, he was no longer worthy of their love** and devotion if he could not be the provider of the finances.

In Breadwinner Annette's interview, she witnessed her mate undergo a complete personality change. Her husband **went from outspoken to introverted and withdrawn once he** lost his employment. He eventually became detached from **household decision-making, leaving his wife to pick up the** pieces. "I think he just gave up. He's a very [proud] person and [when] he was not in control, he just stepped away from the situation." Eventually, the couple separated. Annette's **husband never seemed to fully recover from his inability to** find employment. The husbands of both Annette and Donna had behavior patterns that raised suspicion for underlying **clinical depression, a long-term illness that is commonly un-**diagnosed in the community. In hindsight, if both husbands **had visited a professional therapist, they may have received** the help needed for a full psychological recovery. If those **husbands had received professional assistance, it is possible** that these marriages could have been saved.

More damaging mantrums include infidelity, which can shake the average marriage to its very core. A man who perceives a loss of control in the marriage may seek validation in the arms of another woman, particularly if she is less educated and less accomplished than he. Only one breadwinner was forthright in admitting that infidelity had been an issue in her marriage. Monica admitted why trust was an issue in her marriage: "My husband had an affair with someone who thought he was God's gift. He felt that I was always too busy, so he found someone whom he felt appreciated him."

Unlike the other types of behavior, infidelity is one man**trum that will, of course, never be openly exhibited to the** wife. However, it is one of the most detrimental to the marriage. When feelings of frustration and disempowerment **cause a man to forsake his marital vows, it threatens the** very solvency of the marriage and family.

The last and most damaging forms of mantrum revealed in the interviews was physical aggression and abuse. Regardless of the feelings behind the actions, physical aggression **toward a woman and family is never an acceptable outburst** or expression. Such behavior is a clear indicator of a psycho**logical illness on the part of the husband that was in place** long before the wife became breadwinner. This type of behavior should never be tolerated, no matter how angry he is and regardless of the circumstances. No woman deserves to be subjected to physical aggression and violence because of her salary or any other reason. The harsh reality is that these behaviors will not subside or disappear, regardless of a wife's attempts to pacify her mate. Donna and Helen both endured **physical aggression at the hands of their husbands—both** marriages eventually ended in divorce.

No amount of frustration warrants a physical display of aggression. If this pattern of behavior is present in your marriage, recognize that you deserve better. If you need help, call the National Domestic Violence Hotline at 1-800-799-SAFE or visit the website on a secure computer at www.thehotline.org.

The patterns of behavior discussed in this chapter must first be recognized for what they truly are: forms of displaced anger and expressions of disempowerment. Female breadwinners who become targets of such expressions must find ways to deflect this behavior in their marriages. These ineffective coping mechanisms displayed by the husband are not only psychologically unhealthy for him, they are equally damaging to the wife's psyche. Female breadwinners must refrain from internalizing their husbands' frustration because such actions can leave her feeling guilty and inadequate. Wives should not feel responsible for their husband's happiness or self-esteem—each of us must create that for ourselves. Verbal insults, passive aggression, infidelity, and physical abuse can have lasting emotional and psychological effects on both partners. If such behaviors become commonplace in a marriage, wives must discover ways to save themselves—possibilities can include better communication, professional counseling, or dissolution of the union. Otherwise, they may risk peril at the hands of a maladjusted mate who may be incapable of sustaining a healthy relationship, regardless of any efforts she may put forth.

Closing Thoughts
Where Do We Go From Here?

A CONVERSATION INVOLVES AN INTELLECTUAL exchange between individuals but will only be deemed successful if each side has had a chance to speak candidly and be heard. Dilemmas can be solved only after each **party has had the opportunity to be open and honest about** their needs. The topic of this book is a new one in the culture of American relationships. This book addresses a new frontier in the history of the marriage and the American family: Female Breadwinners. This uncustomary phenomenon is **becoming increasingly prevalent, but most of us are failing** to give it the importance that it deserves. My hope is that this book will serve as a catalyst, initiating honest dialogue between the sexes. If the concepts within these pages inspire couples to engage in effective communication, then I have done what I set out to do.

So the question becomes: What happens when those previously labeled as the "weaker sex" take on a more dominant role in the marriage as the breadwinner? **Some answers may lie within the pages of this book—the remainder will** require the male perspective. I have given female breadwinners a platform on which to speak, and now we are ready to receive. I am not the expert on this topic. I am a student on a journey—a journey toward truth and understanding. My next stop: the men's tent! Communication begins now...

> *Men who may be willing to share their experience in a marriage with a female breadwinner for my next book, please contact me at: menstent@shemakesmore.com.*

Bringing About Healthy Change
A Word from Licensed Mental Health Counselor, Miriam Henry, MA, LMHC

AS YOU READ THE STORIES of the marital challenges of more and more women who are finding success in the workplace, you will see that some of their issues are not surprising. Recent trends suggest that increasing numbers of women will find themselves in similar circumstances. The reasons vary. Disparity in incomes between female **breadwinners and their husbands can create problems in** the psycho-social dynamics of the marriage and family unit. With more and more females being better prepared to com**pete in the workplace, it is predictable that more women will** have similar challenges to face. We are facing a new day with changing values and morals, and you can't solve these problems by pouring new wine into old sheep skin. This book is very timely and will be a stimulus to begin a new conversation between man and wife. Hopefully, such a conversation will heal and restore marital satisfaction.

Unfortunately, many couples missed the opportunity to have pre-martial counseling where couples clarify expectations regarding gender roles, managing finances, desired lifestyle, skills in resolving conflict, child rearing, and the division of labor. This list could go on and on, but the desired **outcome of this process is to give the couple a roadmap of how they want to live their lives together socially,** economically, and spiritually. They would have established common goals that would help them build a successful life together. As I read the women's stories, it's apparent that this has not happened. Many are left relying on their family traditions for gender roles. Men whose mothers took care of the inside of **the home, who witnessed an unstated but understood rule** that it was unmanly to do housework, have difficulty accepting responsibilities related to home management. Adjusting to a new paradigm is not easy for many. However, regardless of one's up-bringing or culture, it's not too late to make the necessary shifts if both husband and wife agree and desire to restore harmony to the marriage if indeed it was ever there.

Here is my recommendation for couples about to get mar**ried:**

> 1) Make pre-marital counseling a must on your to-do list. This service is offered by many church counseling centers, or through private practice counselors. Those who work for companies that have Employee Assistant Programs with a 5-8 session model can utilize this service at no cost.

For those married and struggling with the issues of this change from traditional gender roles in marriage, consider **these thoughts:**

1) No one can force another person to change.

2) You can ask for what you want. Be prepared to hear no.

3) You are not responsible for another person's self-esteem. If it's a problem, the person has to accept responsibility for feeling good about one's self. Everyone has the right to be who they are.

4) With the help of a marriage counselor, you can renegotiate the unspoken marriage contract if it is no longer working.

5) One may need help in balancing work and family life. Many work places are not family friendly so this is an additional stress.

6) Earning high wages is not necessarily the measure of success. Often it's how we use our individual gifts that counts the most.

7) Counseling will help you recognize what your **needs are and how each of you can support each** other.

8) There are marriages that are very satisfying in

spite of income disparity and yours can be, too, if there is willingness by both spouses to work towards trust, honesty, and fulfillment.

Good communication, which is honest and open, is essential for healthy problem-solving. Perhaps some wives/husbands have attempted to talk to spouses about their unhappiness and gotten nowhere. To start a new conversation:

1) Determine a time that doesn't interfere with favorite activities (i.e. television, sports, engagement in any activities). Agree on a time to talk.

2) Avoid using judgmental statements like: "You are so lazy and selfish." Remember, no name calling.

3) Express what you're feeling rather than judgmental thoughts. These old tactics are sure to lead to an unproductive argument.

4) Begin the conversation with a statement of how much the person and the relationship mean to you. Then express your concerns, making a statement such as: "When I come home from work and the house is cluttered and dinner has not been started and you are sitting looking at TV, I feel so discouraged, frustrated, and angry. I feel unsupported and helpless. Our home **and our marriage is not working for either of**

us. I would feel so much better if you would
_____. Are you willing to do some of
these things to help improve our family life?"

5) End your conversation with more words of appreciation.

If these conversations begin a new dialogue, schedule weekly meetings to continue them. Focus on his needs and expectations as well as yours. Agree on ways needs can be met. If this approach doesn't help and you fall back into old patterns of blaming and arguing, it is definitely time the seek help from a professional. Make the appointment and ask your spouse to go with you. If he or she refuses, then go alone. You may find additional resources to help with improving communication at www.nathancobb.com; www.realhope.com; www.livestrong.com; and jdmcounselor.com. Remember, there is help and hope, so reach out and use it.